A GOURMET'S BOOK OF
SHELLFISH

A GOURMET'S BOOK OF

SHELLFISH

MARY CADOGAN

Photographed by
DAVID GILL

Published by Salamander Books Limited
LONDON • NEW YORK

Published 1990 by Salamander Books Ltd
129-137 York Way, London N7 9LG
United Kingdom

This book was created by Merehurst Limited
Ferry House, 51/57 Lacy Road, London SW15 1PR

© 1990 Salamander Books Ltd

ISBN: 0 86101 435 9

Distributed by Hodder and Stoughton Services,
PO Box 6, Mill Road, Dunton Green,
Sevenoaks, Kent TN13 2XX

Commissioned and Directed by Merehurst Limited
Managing Editor: Janet Illsley
Photographer: David Gill
Designer: Sue Storey
Editor: Maureen Callis
Stylist: Maria Kelly
Home Economists: Mary Cadogan and Maxine Clark
Assistant Home Economists: Jaqueline Clark and
Deirdre Shillaker
Typeset by Angel Graphics, London
Colour reproduction by
Scantrans Pte Ltd, Singapore
Printed in Belgium by
Proost International Book Production, Turnhout

ACKNOWLEDGEMENTS
The publishers would like to thank the following for
their help and advice:
Jo Fish at HJ Brunning Ltd, 110 Wandsworth Bridge Rd,
London SW6; Alberto at Penbra Ltd, Unit 6, Rosemary
Rd, Swan Centre, London SW17; Linwoods Fishmonger,
Leadenhall Market, London EC3; R. W. Larkins at
Billingsgate Fish Market, West India Dock Rd, London E14;
Vin Sullivan of Abergavenny, Triley Mill, Abergavenny,
Gwent; Salem Shellfish Scotland Ltd, Unit 3, Blar Mho
Industrial Estate, Fort William, Inverness-shire.

COMPANION VOLUMES OF INTEREST:
A Gourmet's Book of HERBS & SPICES
A Gourmet's Book of CHEESE
A Gourmet's Book of FRUIT
A Gourmet's Book of VEGETABLES
A Gourmet's Book of CHOCOLATE
A Gourmet's Book of TEA & COFFEE
A Gourmet's Book of MUSHROOMS & TRUFFLES

Contents

NOTES FOR RECIPE USERS

Quantities are given in metric, imperial and Australian cups.
Use one set of measures only; they are not interchangeable.

All spoon measures are level: 1 tablespoon = 15 ml spoon;
1 teaspoon = 5 ml spoon.

Use fresh herbs unless otherwise suggested.

All recipes are suitable to serve as a main dish or fish course except where
otherwise indicated at the end of the recipe.

Australian users, note spring onions are the variety commonly termed 'green
shallots' or simply 'shallots' in Australia. Where a recipe specifies shallot, use
a 'brown shallot'.

Introduction

The world of shellfish must surely be one of the most exciting for the gourmet cook. Crustaceans, molluscs and edible sea creatures of all kinds show off their wondrous shapes and colours and, as fishing and transport become more sophisticated, so the variety available increases. As the seasons change it seems there is always something new to inspire us. Shellfish are however surrounded in mystery. Which part of a crab is edible, how do I check a mussel is really fresh, what is the best way to tackle an octopus? These and many other questions are answered in this book.

Here you will find all the main shellfish varieties clearly photographed with a wealth of information about each. Step-by-step photography guides you through preparation and cooking techniques to give you confidence to deal with the shellfish you may wish to cook.

The dictionary describes a gourmet as a 'judge of good eating'. Where shellfish are concerned I feel that the simple approach is usually the best. A few well chosen ingredients, lovingly cooked and carefully presented, are all that you need to enhance the subtle tastes and delicate textures of shellfish. What could be simpler than a delicious grilled lobster strewn with herbs and green peppercorns, or a steaming plate of mussels with aromatic juices just waiting to be mopped up? These are truly gourmet feasts. I hope that you will feel inspired to try them and the many other recipes in this book.

Razor shell clam

Molluscs

Molluscs are invertebrates, protected by a strong outer shell. They can be classified into *Gastropoda* – creatures living in single shells – and *Lamellibranchiata* or bivalves – those with double hinged shells.

Gastropoda include limpets, cockles, whelks and winkles. They are a small, modest group of creatures, not renowned for their great eating qualities. The mirex, also called *escargot de mer*, is a member of this group too; although its eating qualities are poor, it is the source of a purple dye thought to have been discovered by Heracles. The empty mirex shell is a popular home for the hermit crab.

Bivalves are a much larger group and include oysters, clams, mussels, scallops, abalone and razor shells. Many of the molluscs in this group are caught in great abundance, but tend to be ignored. The oyster alone does not suffer neglect – its subtle flavour is renowned the world over.

Molluscs tend to be estuary-or shore-dwelling creatures. Bivalves, such as mussels and oysters, are often found clinging to rocks at the mouth of rivers. As they cannot move voluntarily they usually stay on the same rock for the whole of their lives. Cockles, winkles and whelks can leap short distances and they move with the tide in their thousands. Clams and cockles are usually harvested from beaches at low tide.

Molluscs are usually eaten raw or very briefly cooked. They must therefore be very fresh. Mussels, oysters and clams are usually sold live. Their shells must be tightly closed and any that are open should be tapped sharply; if the shell closes they are fine to eat; if it remains open the shellfish is dead and must be discarded.

Because molluscs such as mussels and clams tend to live in shallow sandy waters, they tend to take sand and other particles into their shell when they feed. When placed in a bucket of cold salted water with a sprinkling of oatmeal or flour, the fish will feed on the oatmeal and excrete the dirt. Scrub the mollusc shell thoroughly using a stiff brush to remove grit and barnacles.

Oysters are usually eaten raw, in the half shell with their juices. Cockles and razor shells can also be eaten raw and are often sprinkled with lemon juice or vinegar. Most other molluscs are cooked before eating. Mussels and clams are usually steamed in their own juices, but they are also delicious baked and stuffed, or used in soups and stews. The delicate flavoured scallop requires careful cooking to protect its soft texture. It is often poached or steamed and served with a creamy sauce.

Cockles, winkles and whelks are generally sold cooked. Serve them cold with vinegar and brown bread and butter in the traditional style of the true Londoner.

Selection of molluscs: oysters, cockles, whelks, scallops, clams, mussels and winkles

Clam

Clams are available throughout the year but are at their best in the autumn. There are more clam species available in North America than Europe and they are extremely popular in America, particularly the soft-shell and hard-shell clams. Many of the American clams have European relatives, but they are less popular in Britain.

The soft-shell clam (*Mya arenaria*), also called longneck or steamer, is harvested from the White Sea to North Carolina in the west and to Britain and France in the east. The shell is dirty fawn or white.

Soft shell clams have thin, brittle shells with a gap at each end. Because of this, they are often sandy and gritty and need particularly thorough cleaning (see below).

The hard-shell clam (*Mercenaria mercenaria*), also known as quahog or littleneck, originally came from North America, but has become colonized in many places around the Mediterranean and Ireland. It has an oval shell which is dull grey or brown outside and purple inside.

The surf or bar clam (*Spisula solidissima*), native to North America, is a large clam up to 15 cm (6 in) across with a smooth creamy brown shell. Because of its size it is usually chopped or minced for use in chowders, or sliced and deep-fried.

The wedge shell (*Donax trunculus*) is plentiful in the Mediterranean. This small clam is closely related to some American species, including the bean clam (*Donax spp.*). The shell may be white, yellow, purple or brown.

The carpet shell (*Venerupis decussata*), is a small clam up to 8 cm (3 in) across. It is white, yellow or light brown and a native of Britain and the Mediterranean. It is excellent and much sought after. It can be eaten raw like an oyster. The smaller golden carpet shell (*Venerupis aurea*) is also popular.

The venus shell (*Callista chione*) has a smooth shiny reddish brown decorative shell. It is caught from southern Britain to the Mediterranean and is similar to the carpet shell, although a little larger. It can be cooked or eaten raw.

The smaller warty venus (*Venus verrucosa*) is caught in the same waters and is greatly appreciated in Mediterranean countries. This clam is called *vongola* in Italy and is the one used in the famous *vongole* sauce for pasta.

Buying and Storing

Because clams are cooked only briefly or eaten raw, they must be absolutely fresh when you buy them. They are sold live in the shell and should be eaten within 24 hours. Put them in a bucket of clean water with a sprinkling of oatmeal or cornmeal, leave for 24 hours, then scrub shells under running cold water with a stiff brush. Discard any with broken or gaping shells.

Preparation

To open a clam, use a strong sharp knife to prise the shell open and sever the hinge. Discard the top shell if serving raw. If you want to remove the clam completely from the shell, insert the point of the knife between the clam and the shell and cut the clam free. Pick out any pieces of broken shell and wash the clam thoroughly.

To cook clams in the shell, put in a large saucepan with enough water just to cover the bottom of the pan. Cover tightly and cook for 3-8 minutes, depending on size and number of clams, shaking the pan occasionally, until the shells have opened. Discard any that haven't.

Serving Suggestions

Clams are usually steamed like mussels in their own juices, and the liquor served as a broth to dip bread or the clams into. They are often eaten raw like oysters, too.

They are particularly good in soups and chowders; baked and stuffed in the half shell; used in sauces to serve with rice or pasta; battered and deep-fried; or in pies.

Clams can also be used in any recipe calling for mussels or oysters, although they do not have such a fine flavour as oysters.

Hard-shell clam (large)

Littleneck clam

Quahog clam

Soft-shell clam

Warty Venus clam

Carpet shell clam

Golden carpet shell clam

Mussel

The mussel is a familiar sight in fish stalls and markets throughout the autumn and winter. Often called the poor man's oyster it provides a delicious meal at relatively low cost. The name mussel is derived from the latin word *mus* meaning mousse, perhaps because of its shape.

The thin crescent-shaped shell of the common mussel (*Mytilus edulis*) is usually dark blue or blackish, but some varieties can be paler with dark brown or purple markings. The mussels cling in clusters to rocks, although commercially they are more likely to be hanging from ropes attached to stakes in mussel farms.

Musselburgh, in Scotland, once the site of a Roman camp, owes its name to the mussel beds located at the mouth of the river Esk.

Mussels sold commercially are collected from waters that are known to be clean, although they should still be carefully washed before eating. An area around the north Norfolk coastline from Brancaster to Blakeney is the only EEC pollution-free harbour in Britain where mussel farming is allowed. From May onwards the mussel spawn is collected from the sandbanks and taken to holding pits where they are left to fatten in the clear water. It is inadvisable to collect mussels in the wild as they may be affected by pollution.

Mussels are generally sold live in the shell, but they are also available frozen, in or out of the shell; canned or in jars in brine; or sometimes fresh, cooked and shelled.

Cultivated mussels vary in size, colour and flavour and there is great disagreement about where the best flavoured mussel comes from. They are cultivated extensively in France, Spain, the Netherlands and along the American Atlantic coastline.

The New Zealand greenlip mussel (*Perna canalicula*) is large and has a particularly rich flavour. It is available fresh, frozen or bottled in Australia and New Zealand.

The horse mussel (*Modiolus modiolus*) is another large mussel, harvested in the North Atlantic. The shell is purplish-yellow and the flesh is orange. It does not have such a good flavour as the common mussel and is best used in robustly flavoured sauces.

The fan mussel (*Pinna fragilis*, var. *Pinna pectinata*), also called pen shell or sea wing, is the largest of the British bivalves and can measure over 35 cm (14 in) across. The yellow-brown shell has a pointed end which it buries in the sand. It can be cooked like a scallop.

Buying and Storing
When buying live mussels, check the shells are tightly closed. Open shells indicate that the fish inside is dead and should not be eaten. Store for up to 24 hours in a bucket of cold water in a cool place. Discard any that have opened or that float at the end of this time.

If time allows, sprinkle a little oatmeal or flour on the water: the mussels will feed on the oatmeal and excrete their dirt.

Preparation
Scrub shells thoroughly and remove any barnacles or weed with a strong knife. Pull off the fibrous beard attached to each shell. Rinse again in clear water. Discard any that are open and do not close when tapped sharply, and any with damaged shells.

To cook, put mussels in a large saucepan with a little water or wine. Cover and cook for 3-5 minutes, depending on size and number of mussels, until shells have opened; discard any that do not open.

Serving Suggestions
Mussels are most often steamed in their own juices or with wine and garlic *à la marinière*.

After the preparatory cooking described above they can also be wrapped in bacon and grilled; baked in the open shell with parsley, breadcrumbs and garlic, or pesto, or tomato sauce; added to soups; mixed with tomato sauce and served with pasta; and used with other fish and shellfish in seafood casseroles.

Mussels can also be used as a substitute for clams.

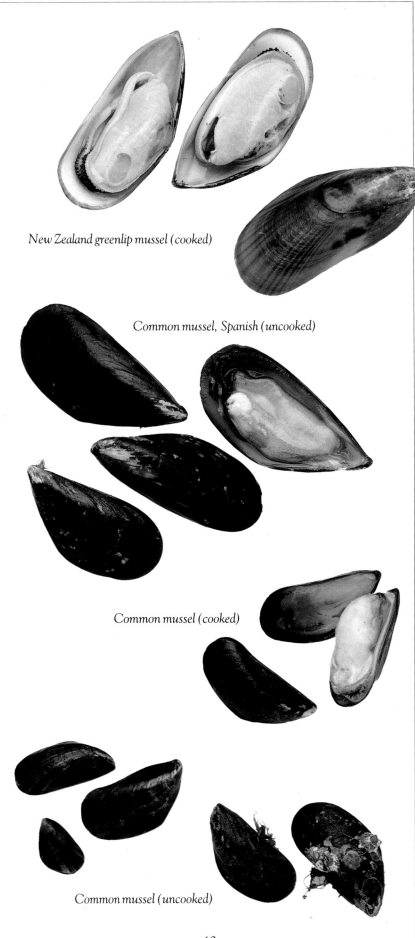

New Zealand greenlip mussel (cooked)

Common mussel, Spanish (uncooked)

Common mussel (cooked)

Common mussel (uncooked)

Oyster

Until the 19th century oysters were an everyday food eaten by the poor to eke out expensive meat. But because of over-fishing they are now comparatively rare and have become a luxury seafood with a high price. The culture of oysters can be traced back to classical times; shells have been found in the ancient ruins of Roman times when they were fattened in tanks and cultured to ensure a good supply.

The European oyster (*Ostrea edulis*) is considered to have the best flavour, with the English native oyster being the most prized. It has a greyish brown, irregular shell, reaching up to 11 cm (4 in).

The Colchester oyster feast is an annual ceremony of ancient origin. Oysters grown around Mersea Island are gathered and consumed at the feast on the last Friday of October. Around 2000 oysters are consumed by invited guests, washed down with a glass of Guinness.

European oysters are found from the Norwegian sea down to the Mediterranean and Morocco. They are cultured in many places, notably Whitstable in Kent, Colchester in Essex, Marennes-Oleron and Auray in France, Ostend in Belgium and Zeeland in the Netherlands. These oysters are best served raw in the half shell with just a squeeze of lemon juice.

The less worthy Portuguese oyster (*Crassostrea angulata*) is elongated, reaching up to 17 cm (6½ in). Although it can be eaten raw, it is not as good as the European oyster and is therefore best used in cooked dishes.

On the American side of the Atlantic, you will find the American or Eastern oyster (*Crassostrea virginica*). This species has a rough greyish shell and reaches 17 cm (6½ in) in length. It is relatively abundant and is used in a wide variety of ways, including soups, stews and bakes.

The giant Pacific oyster (*Crassostrea gigas*) is a large oyster from the Orient which can reach 25 cm (10 in) in length. It has been successfully introduced to several areas of the North Atlantic. It is also called the Japanese Oyster.

The most popular oyster farmed in Australia is the Sydney rock oyster (*Saccostrea commercialis*).

Buying and Storing

Oysters are not normally available during the summer months, when spawning makes them appear fatter, as they contain eggs, and they are less succulent to eat.

Oysters are sold by the dozen in the shell or half shell. If bought in the shell, they should be live with the shells tightly closed; discard any that do not close when tapped – this means they are dead. If bought in the half shell, they should be plump, a natural creamy colour with clear shiny liquid and a pleasant sea smell. They should be eaten on the day of purchase.

Oysters can also be bought in jars and cans, smoked or unsmoked.

Preparation

If bought in the shell, scrub under running cold water to remove the sand.

To open an oyster, hold firmly in absorbent kitchen paper or a napkin on a work surface, with the flatter shell uppermost and hinged end towards you. Insert the point of an oyster knife into the gap in the hinge linking the shells. Twist knife blade firmly to snap the shells apart.

Work knife along inside of upper shell to sever muscle holding the shells together. Discard top shell, retaining as much liquid in lower shell as possible.

To free the oyster, work knife under oyster to cut through muscle holding it to lower shell.

Serving Suggestions

Allow 6 to 12 oysters per person and serve on a bed of cracked ice, with lemon. Oysters are also very good wrapped in bacon and grilled; sprinkled with breadcrumbs and parsley and lightly grilled; or stuffed with spinach and cooked, as Oysters Rockefeller (see page 65).

Smoked oysters are good as part of a starter, a garnish and in salads.

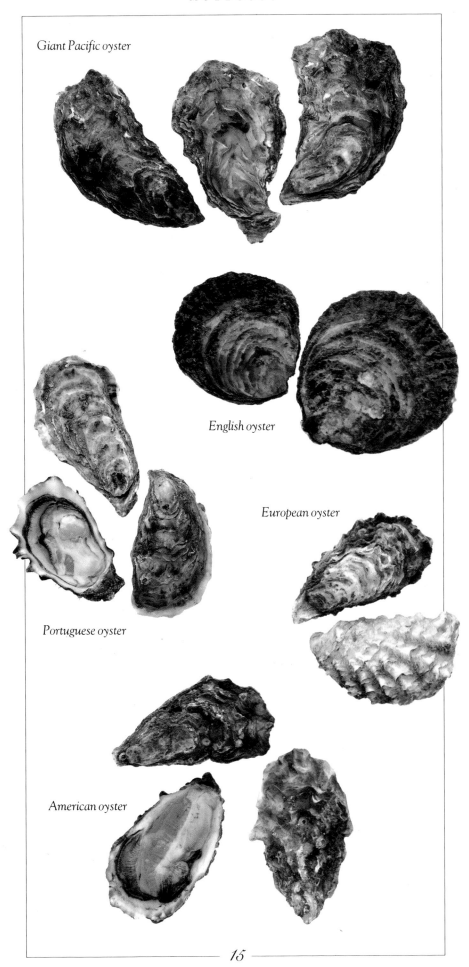

Giant Pacific oyster

English oyster

European oyster

Portuguese oyster

American oyster

Scallop

Scallops are among the most sought after seafood. They have a delectable flavour and soft texture. Available throughout the winter, they are at their best during the coldest months.

Scallops swim around by opening and closing their shells to propel themselves through the water. The white muscle joining the upper and lower shells is therefore relatively large and powerful.

Most scallops are hermaphrodites, each containing an orange roe (or coral) and whitish testis. Their fan-shaped ridged shell makes an attractive container for seafood starters; Coquille St Jacques is baked in the shells.

The edible part is the large white muscle and the coral attached to it, although in America the coral is not normally eaten. All other parts, including the frilly mantle surrounding the muscle, are discarded. This initial preparation is usually done by the fishmongers.

The great scallop (*Pecten maximus*), or king scallop, is the most common variety. It has a pinkish or whitish brown shell, up to 15 cm (6 in) in diameter.

The queen scallop (*Pecten opercularis*), is a small scallop with an almost circular shell. It is found in deeper waters than the great scallop and fishing for it is a comparatively new development. The roe is usually a vivid orange red.

Both of these scallops are fished around British waters. They are particularly popular in the Isle of Man where they are called 'Tan rogan'. They can be eaten throughout the year but are at their fattest and best from January to June. There are about 8 large scallops and approximately 40 queen scallops or 'queenies', as they are often called, to 500 g (1 lb).

Another smaller relative of the great scallop is the pétoncle (*Chlamys varia*). It has a firmer muscle, which is not as white.

The Bay scallop (*Argopecten irradians*) is another small scallop which is fished commercially off the American Atlantic coast. It is a great delicacy and can be eaten raw when very fresh. The larger saucer scallop (*Amusium balloti*) is a popular Australian species.

Buying and Storing
When buying in the complete shell, select only those scallops that are tightly closed. Scrub the shells under running cold water and leave to stand in a bucket of cold salted water for an hour to cleanse themselves. Eat within 24 hours.

More usually, scallops are sold in the half shell, cleaned and ready to cook. Look for white meat with no discoloration and a plump coral. Consume on the day of purchase.

Scallops are also available shelled and frozen, often without the coral. They should be thawed slowly, to retain their flavour and texture, then cooked as soon as possible.

Preparation
To open the shell, hold the scallop in a cloth with the flat shell uppermost. Insert a small sharp knife into the small opening between the shells and carefully work it across the inside of the flat shell to sever the muscle. Prise the shells apart. To free the scallop, carefully slide the knife blade under the greyish outer rim of the scallop (this is the mantle). Remove the flesh from the shell and separate the white muscle and orange coral; remove any dark strands with the point of a sharp knife and discard the mantle and other organs. Rinse the muscle and coral and scrub the inside of the deep shell if it is to be used as a cooking vessel.

Serving Suggestions
Scallops need careful cooking to preserve their delicate taste and texture; overcooking renders them tough and rubbery. They are best poached or steamed, but can also be fried or baked under a cheese sauce – as for Coquille St Jacques.

Scallops are also delicious sautéed briefly in garlic butter and sprinkled with herbs; or wrapped in bacon, sprinkled with lime juice and grilled to perfection.

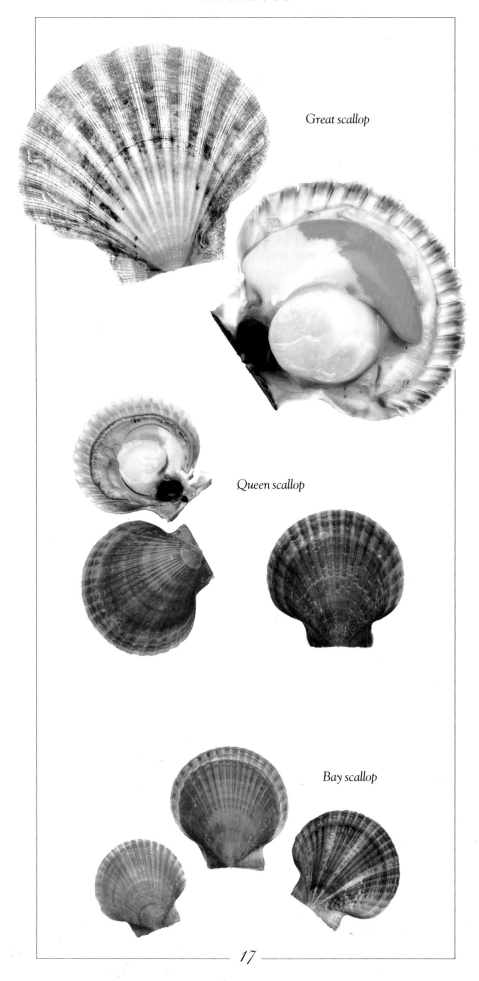

Great scallop

Queen scallop

Bay scallop

Abalone

The abalone (*Haliotis tuberculata*) or ormer has other common names, including mutton fish, earshell, sea ears and paua (in New Zealand). Abalone used to play an important part in the diet of Aborigines in Australia and Maoris in New Zealand.

The species is called ormer in Britain and the Mediterranean and abalone in new world countries. The best abalone are thought to be those caught on the Pacific Coast of North America. In Britain the ormer is found only in the Channel Islands.

The abalone is bigger than an oyster, with a maximum length of 13 cm (5 in). It is as renowned for its beautiful pearly shell, which is used to make jewellery and ornaments, as for the fish itself. It is said you can tell the age of an abalone by the number of small holes found along the curved edge of the shell.

When the shell is opened it reveals a round white muscle, known as the foot, surrounded by a darker coloured frilly muscle called the mantle. The foot is the part which is commonly eaten. The meat needs to be tenderized by beating before being braised or fried.

The main species are the blacklip abalone (*Haliotis ruber*) and the greenlip abalone (*Haliotis laevigata*). The blacklip abalone has a red corrugated shell and is given its name because of the black mantle that surrounds the foot. It lives in crevices, caves and coastal reefs. The greenlip abalone has a red shell streaked with light green and is roughly corrugated. It lives on open rock faces and is said to be the most tender.

Buying and Storing

Abalone can be bought live or dead in the shell. Buy live ones if possible as the fresher they are the more tender they will be. To check if one is alive, touch the meat and it will move.

Live abalone can be kept fresh for up to 2 days in a bucket of salted water covered with a damp cloth. If buying dead abalone, remove from the shell immediately and store, wrapped, in the refrigerator for up to 24 hours.

Preparation

To shell abalone, force the tip of an oyster knife (or other small strong knife) into the thin end of the shell underneath the flesh. Work the blade until the muscle becomes free. Remove the white foot and wash thoroughly. Discard the intestine. The foot may be left whole or cut into thin slices. To tenderize, pound the meat with a mallet until limp and velvety.

Serving Suggestions

Whole tenderized abalone is best braised. Slices of abalone can be quickly stir-fried, or coated in egg and breadcrumbs and deep-fried. Finely chopped or minced abalone can be made into fritters or added to soups and chowders. The Chinese sometimes steam abalone in the shell for as long as 10 hours to tenderize.

To cook abalone in the shell, return tenderized meat to cleaned shell, top with grated ginger, chilli strips and oyster sauce; steam for about 2 hours.

Ocean Quahog

The ocean quahog (*Arctica islandica*) is similar in appearance to the quahog clam (see page 10) but it is not the same species. It is almost circular in shape with a brown-black shell and lives in fairly deep water in sandy mud. It is found from Newfoundland to North Carolina and in European waters, although it is not generally fished in the latter.

The flavour varies greatly according to habitat; some can have a strong unpleasant taste. The flesh is dark, making it unsuitable for use in clam chowders and creamy sauces. Ocean quahog is mainly used in America, in minced clam products and stews.

Abalone

Ocean Quahog

Cockle

The cockle (*Cerastaderma edule*) is made up of two ridged oval shells hinged by a ligament at the pointed end. The shell can be brown, pale yellow or off-white and it reaches a maximum size of 6 cm (2½ in) across. Cockles are at their best in winter and are usually sold cooked, with or without their shell.

Cockles are often found on the beach, especially at low tide. They are a common sight around the beaches of Britain, particularly in Norfolk and the West Country.

Cerastaderma edule is an inhabitant of British waters; *Cerastaderma glaucum*, in the Mediterranean, is almost identical. Relatives of these include the larger spiny cockle (*Acanthocardia aculeata*), the prickly cockle (*Acanthocardia echinata*) and *Acanthocardia tuberculata*, called *cuore rossa* in Italy because the animal in the shell is bright red when alive. The dog cockle (*Glycymeris glycymeris*), with its distinctive patterned shell, is found throughout the Mediterranean.

In all there are over 200 varieties of cockle found throughout the world, not all of them worth eating.

The heart shell or heart cockle (*Glossus humanus*) is not a true cockle but looks very similar; it is heart-shaped when viewed sideways. It is found from Iceland and Norway down to the Mediterranean.

Buying and Storing
If you harvest the cockles yourself or buy them live, clean carefully before cooking. Leave them in a bucket of lightly salted water for 1 hour to rid them of sand. Discard any that are not tightly closed. Scrub the shells under running cold water. Live cockles can be kept in a bucket of salted water for up to 24 hours.

Cockles are most often sold ready cooked, either in or out of their shell. The streets of London used to throng with stalls selling cockles dressed with vinegar, but they are now a rare sight, except in some seaside towns.

Preparation
In Britain it is usual to steam cockles briefly in a little water until the shells open, then remove shells and dress the cockles with vinegar.

They can also be poached, grilled, baked or barbecued. Whatever the method, it should take no more than 5 minutes for the shell to open, meaning the cockles are cooked.

Stir-fried cockles are good: shell them as you would an oyster (see page 14), then stir-fry quickly in oil flavoured with garlic and herbs.

Serving Suggestions
Cockles make good sauces for pasta and rice, or they can be used in starters or soups.

Razor Shell Clam

Razor shell clams (*Ensis ensis*) are very distinctive: they have long brittle shells resembling the old-fashioned cut-throat razor – hence their name. They gape permanently at both ends, making them impossible to market because of the health hazard. The shells can grow to a length of 13 cm (5 in) – the creature can protrude from each end. They are found in shallow sandy waters. (Illustrated on page 8.)

Preparation
Cover with salted water and leave to stand for 1 hour to allow them to rid themselves of sand. Remove clams, change the water and repeat.

To cook, put in a large pan with 1 cm (½ in) depth of water or wine. Bring to the boil, cover and shake pan for about 2 minutes, until shells open; discard any that do not. The meat can then be stir-fried, baked, barbecued or poached very briefly; it toughens with overcooking.

Serving Suggestions
Serve on canapés; as starters; in salads; in soups, casseroles and sauces; sauté in flavoured oils; or coat in egg and breadcrumbs and deep-fry. Use in any recipe calling for clams.

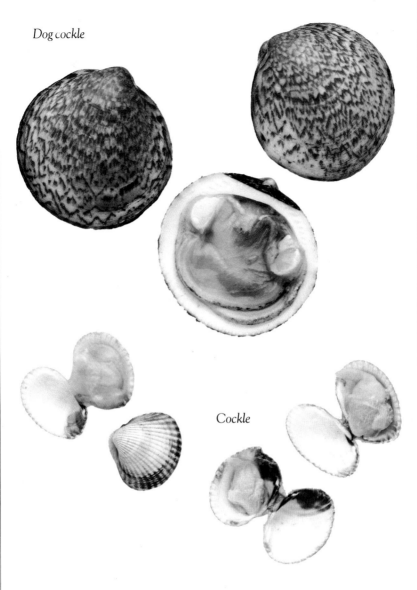

Dog cockle

Cockle

Limpet

Limpets (*Patella vulgata*) are not normally eaten these days. They are rarely seen on sale at fish markets as they are not commercially marketed. Although they are edible and were once quite popular in Britain, they are not particularly tender or good to eat.

Limpets are usually collected off rocks around the British coastline at low tide; January, February and March are said to be the best months to collect them.

The Scots used to mix limpets with oatmeal before cooking, while along the south coast they were piled up on the rocks and covered with burning straw to cook them.

Limpets are small, usually about 5 cm (2 in) across, with a grey, yellowish or brown conical shell which is almost symmetrical. The inside of the shell is pearly.

Limpets found off the coast of North America are even smaller and barely worth eating.

Preparation
To clean, soak limpets in a bucket of lightly salted water for 2-3 hours, then boil for about 10 minutes. They can also be eaten raw or baked briefly with a little butter.

Limpets are probably best used to flavour sauces, or made into stovies Scottish-style.

Winkle

The winkle (*Littorina littorea*), or periwinkle as it is also known, has a small snail-like shell about 2.5 cm (1 in) long. The convoluted shell is usually dark grey or brown.

Like cockles and whelks, winkles are traditionally sold ready cooked from street stalls in London and on seaside promenades. They are usually sold cold, dressed in vinegar. These stalls are a less common sight these days.

Winkles were formerly popular in Northern Ireland where they were called willicks. They were usually extracted from their shells with a pin (called a winkle pick) and dipped in oatmeal before eating.

Winkles have been popular in Europe for centuries and are still often found in the *fruits de mer* platter of coastal towns of Brittany.

Buying and Storing
Winkles are harvested commercially. They are usually sold ready boiled. If bought uncooked, soak for 1 hour in salted water with a sprinkling of oatmeal or flour to rid them of any grit. Take out the winkles, change the water and repeat the process. Cook within 24 hours of purchase.

Preparation
Boil in their shells in salted water or court bouillon (see page 24) for about 5 minutes. Serve in the shell: each diner removes the meat with a winkle pin and seasons it with salt, pepper and vinegar.

Serving Suggestions
Serve as part of a seafood platter for starters or buffets; or as a tasty snack.

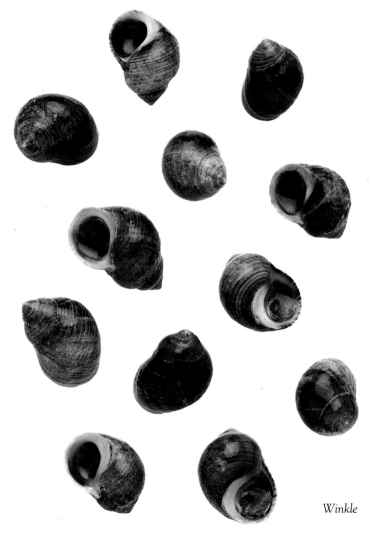

Winkle

Whelk

Whelk

The whelk (*Buccinum undatum*) resembles the winkle as it has a similar snail-like shell, but the whelk is much larger. Whelks often reach 10 cm (4 in) in length; some are as long as 15 cm (6 in). American whelks are even larger; *Busycon carica*, for example, can reach 30 cm (12 in). Like winkles, whelks are traditional London and seaside fare.

The shell of the whelk varies in colour from grey to brown and is often striped. Its lips have great powers of suction and are used to kill other molluscs, sucking out their contents. It is the large muscular foot which is normally eaten, although they can be eaten whole.

Buying and Storing
Whelks are commercially harvested, and this is certainly the best way to obtain them. They are usually sold ready cooked and removed from their shell.

If bought uncooked, soak for 1 hour in salted water with a sprinkling of oatmeal or flour. Change the water and soak again. This purges them of their dirt. Cook as soon as possible, certainly within 24 hours of purchase.

Preparation
Boil uncooked whelks in shells in salted water or court bouillon (see page 24) for about 5 minutes. Remove from their shells with a skewer or fork and dress with salt, pepper and vinegar.

Serving Suggestions
Serve whelks as part of a seafood platter for starters or buffets; marinate in herb dressing and serve with brown bread and butter; bake with garlic butter in the same way as you would snails; add them to omelettes and rice dishes.

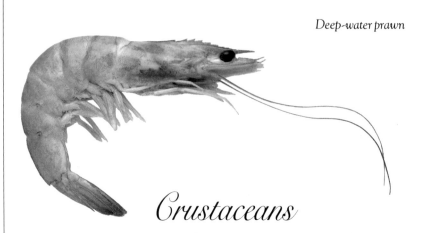

Deep-water prawn

Crustaceans

Crustaceans are shellfish which have an external skeleton. They all have legs and are able to move. Some, like lobsters, have a jointed shell which helps them to move. Crabs do not have a jointed shell but use their legs to scurry about.

Crustaceans are members of the *Arthropoda* family which includes spiders, scorpions and insects. They are covered in a hard horny shell or, more correctly, carapace. This shell is shed periodically as the creature grows – evidence of which can be seen washed up on shorelines. Generally speaking it is a good idea to choose lobsters and crabs whose shells are encrusted and obviously old as the flesh will have had time to develop and fill the shell. A crustacean with a new shell will often be small and lacking in flavour. An exception to this rule is the soft shell crab (see page 40).

Crustaceans range from the tiniest shrimp with its semi-transparent fragile shell, to the large European lobster whose tough shell can often be utilized as a serving dish. Their flesh is firm and sweet, particularly the fine flavoured European lobster and the delicate freshwater crayfish.

Many crustaceans are available all year, but tend to be at their best in the summer. When choosing a large crustacean such as lobster or crab, look for specimens which feel heavy for their size, with legs and claws intact. Ideally, they should be bought live, but if cooked store in the refrigerator and eat as soon as possible – certainly within 24 hours.

Most shellfish have indigestible or inedible parts, such as the gills or 'dead mens fingers' of crabs and lobsters, or the intestinal tract of the king prawn. These must be removed during preparation. The roe, also called coral, and liver, sometimes called tomalley, of the lobster should never be discarded. They are considered delicacies and can be used to make delicate sauces.

The cooking time for all crustaceans tends to be short as the flesh is tender and can become dry very quickly with overcooking. Many change their colour when cooked: the blue-black lobster turns scarlet and the blue-grey king prawn turns pink. Lobsters are usually boiled in salt water or a court bouillon (see below), then served plain or with a sauce.

Small crustaceans such as prawns and king prawns can be deep-fried; they are usually first coated in batter or egg and breadcrumbs to protect their delicate flesh from the heat. They can also be grilled, either marinated first or brushed with butter or oil to keep them moist.

The tiny superbly flavoured brown shrimp is eaten plainly boiled or potted with butter.

Court Bouillon

To a large pan of cold water, add ¼ bottle white wine or wine vinegar, 1 sliced carrot, 1 sliced onion, 1 sliced stick celery, 12 peppercorns, 2 bay leaves, 3 sprigs of parsley and a good sprinkling of salt. Simmer for 20 minutes before adding the shellfish.

Selection of crustaceans: crab, lobster, Dublin Bay prawn, scampi tail, crab claw, king prawn, pink shrimp and brown shrimp

Prawn

Prawns are probably the most well known and popular seafood. They are called shrimps in America. There are two main categories: the common prawn (*Palaemom serratus*) of the *Palaemonidae* family, and the deep-water or Northern prawn (*Pandalus borealis*) of the *Pandalidae* family. There are several related species which are rarely distinguished from each other.

The common prawn is found in shallow in-shore waters. It walks forward, looking for food with its stalked eyes, feeling with its antennae and sweeping the seabed with its second pair of legs. It is fished extensively from Norway down to the Mediterranean. It reaches a maximum length of 9 cm (3½ in) and when alive its shell is almost colourless.

The deep-water prawn is larger with a maximum length of 13 cm (5 in). This prawn is red when alive and is usually cooked at sea, before it reaches the market. Its range extends from Greenland to Britain, with large quantities caught in Norwegian waters.

King prawns belong to the *Penaeidae* family and include the Mediterranean prawn fished off Spain and Portugal. There are also several varieties found in Australia. King prawns can reach lengths of up to 20 cm (8 in). They are usually blue-grey and have succulent meaty flesh. They make good starters, particularly when bought raw and freshly cooked. The most commonly found king prawns are: the *Parapenaeus longirostris*, called the *crevette rose* in France because of its pink colour, which has a maximum length of 16 cm (6 in); *Penaeus kerathurus*, brown with reddish tints, often called *crevette royale* in France, is a little larger, up to 22 cm (9 in); and *Aristeus antennatus* (*crevette rouge* in France), which has a light red body and mauve head and is up to 20 cm (8 in) long. All these species are found in the waters of the Mediterranean.

Other common types include the Eastern king prawn (*Penaeus plebegus*), Western king prawn (*Penaeus latisulcatus*), creamy yellow banana prawn (*Penaeus merguiensis*), and the brown tiger prawn (*Penaeus esculentus*), so called because of its brown and orange striped shell.

In Australia you will find another group of prawns. Two which fall somewhere in size between a deep-water and a king prawn are the school prawn (*Metapenaeus macleayi*), found in rivers and bays, and the greasyback or greentail prawn (*Metapenaeus bennettae*) which is caught mainly in estuaries.

Buying and Storing

Prawns are sold raw (dead, but uncooked) or cooked, shelled or unshelled, whole or headless. Raw prawns should have a firm body, without black traces, and a fresh sea smell. Cooked prawns should have firm flesh with tight shells and no black or loose heads or legs.

Prawns are best eaten on the day of purchase and shelled just before serving to retain moisture. Store in an airtight container in the refrigerator, but eat within 24 hours.

Preparation

To cook raw prawns, plunge them into boiling salted water and simmer for 3-5 minutes, until they have turned pinky red; king prawns will take 6-8 minutes.

To peel prawns, break or cut off the head, then slip off the tail and body shell. Slit king prawns down the centre back with a small sharp knife, then carefully remove the dark intestinal vein. The end of the tail section is often left on, particularly when the prawns are to be grilled or barbecued.

Serving Suggestions

Prawns can be grilled, stir-fried, deep-fried, or baked. Cooked prawns are useful in salads, prawn cocktails and countless starter and main course dishes: prawn risotto, Prawn Satay (page 75), Spicy Chinese Prawns (page 74) and prawn brochettes are just a few examples. When using cooked prawns in a hot dish, reheat carefully to avoid them becoming tough.

Deep-water prawn

Common prawn

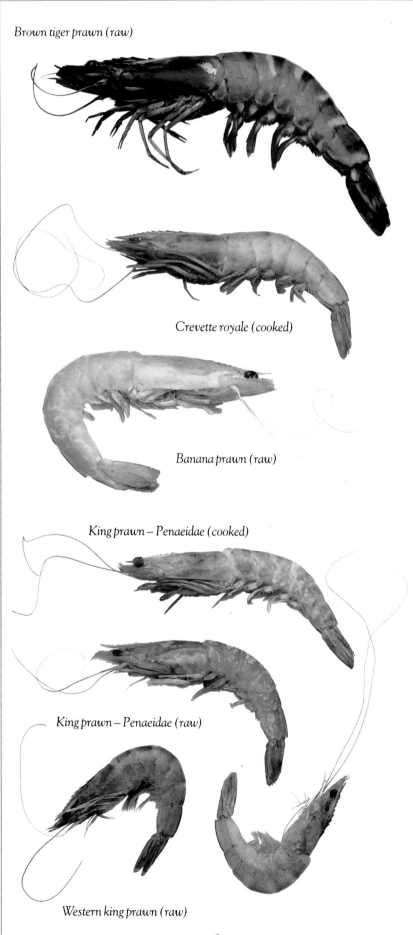

Brown tiger prawn (raw)

Crevette royale (cooked)

Banana prawn (raw)

King prawn – Penaeidae (cooked)

King prawn – Penaeidae (raw)

Western king prawn (raw)

Brown shrimp (cooked)

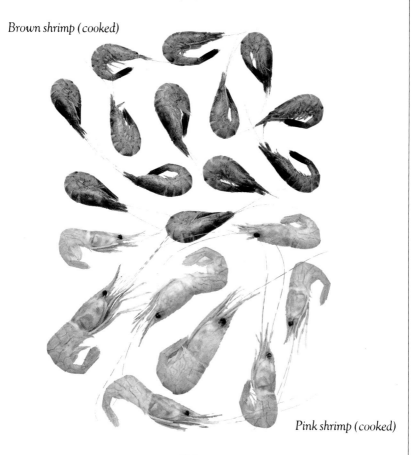

Pink shrimp (cooked)

Shrimp

In Britain the term shrimp describes the brown shrimp (*Crangon crangon*) which, with a maximum length of just 6 cm (2½ in), is the smallest crustacean to be eaten in any quantity. This transluscent little creature lives on sandy ground and can vary its colour from grey to brown to match its surroundings and provide camouflage.

Shrimps commonly found in the United States: the American brown shrimp (*Penaeus aztecus aztecus*), pink shrimp (*Penaeus duorarum duorarum*) and white shrimp (*Penaeus setiferus*) are much larger. They can vary in size from 5-15 cm (2-6 in) and are more closely related to the king prawn. They are fished south of the Carolinas.

Buying and Storing
Shrimps are available all year round and are usually sold ready boiled, either shelled or unshelled. If bought uncooked they are usually dead so should be cooked as soon as possible: boil in salted water for 3 minutes, or until they turn pinky brown; leave to cool in the water.

Shrimps are best eaten on the day of purchase. Store, unpeeled, in a plastic bag or airtight container in the refrigerator until required.

Preparation
To peel, hold the shrimp between two fingers, then gently pull off the tail shell and twist off the head.

Serving Suggestions
Shrimps are sold mostly as potted shrimps: the tail meat is removed and potted with butter and spices, usually mace and nutmeg. They make an excellent snack or starter.

Serve cold cooked shrimps as a starter in their shell. Provide finger bowls and serve with thinly sliced brown bread and butter.

The flavour of the shrimp is excellent and makes a particularly good addition to creamy rice or pasta dishes, stuffings for fish fillets, such as sole or plaice, or little moulds to serve as starters.

Dublin Bay Prawn

The Dublin Bay prawn (*Nephrops norvegicus*) is also called Norway Lobster in some parts of Britain. It is the same species as the langoustine, featured on so many French seaside menus, and the scampi, so often battered or egg-and-crumbed and frozen.

This crustacean is rose-grey or pink in colour and can reach up to 25 cm (10 in) in length. It is found most commonly in the Adriatic and west and central parts of the Mediterranean.

Dublin Bay prawns are so called not because they are caught in the Bay, but because fishing boats often came into Dublin Bay having caught the shellfish accidentally along with their catch. They would then sell them off the boats to Dublin street vendors.

Buying and Storing

In the Mediterranean, Dublin Bay prawns are usually sold in their shells, live or cooked. In Britain they are more commonly sold as frozen tails, but are becoming more widely available whole, either live or cooked.

They are often sold as scampi, though correctly this name should be used only for the large prawns from the Bay of Naples. Scampi is available ready cooked or frozen.

Live Dublin Bay prawns should be evenly coloured with no black discoloration. Look for a firm body and pleasant sea smell. Store in a damp hessian bag for up to 24 hours.

Cooked Dublin Bay prawns should have firm flesh, no missing or black limbs and a pleasant sea smell. Leave in the shell until needed as this keeps the flesh succulent. Store in the refrigerator and eat within 24 hours of purchase.

Preparation

Cook live Dublin Bay prawns in boiling salted water for 10-12 minutes, depending on size.

To shell, twist off the head then gently pull off the tail shell and remove the body shell. Cut down the back and remove the dark vein.

Serving Suggestions

These shellfish can be eaten hot or cold. They are often served as a starter, cold with mayonnaise or hot with melted butter or warm hollandaise sauce.

They may be coated in egg and breadcrumbs and deep-fried, or cooked in a wine sauce to serve with rice. They are particularly good with spicy sauces, such as sweet and sour or creole sauce.

Mantis Shrimp

This unusual looking creature is related to the crab, but looks much more like a prawn. It grows to a maximum length of 25 cm (10 in) and has a yellowish-green shell. It has five pairs of legs; the front pair serve as extensions to the mouth and the next pair are used to grasp food. This action resembles that of the praying mantis, hence its name.

The mantis shrimp (*Squilla empusa*) is found in mud holes around the eastern seaboard of the United States. Its European relative *Squilla mantis* is brown-grey in colour and is mainly found in the waters of Spain, France and Portugal.

Mantis shrimp are rarely available in European and American markets, except around the Mediterranean.

Preparation and Serving

In the Mediterranean region, mantis shrimp are often used in fish soups and stocks. Or they may be boiled or steamed and then shelled and eaten like king prawns.

Dublin Bay prawn (cooked)

Lobster

The European lobster (*Homarus gammarus*) and the American lobster (*Homarus americanus*) are similar in appearance, but the American is larger. The European lobster is found from the far north to the Mediterranean. The American lobster is found as far south as South Carolina.

Lobsters can only be caught in special lobster pots and this is one of the reasons for their high cost. They are available throughout the year but are at their best during the summer.

As with other crustaceans, a lobster will shed its shell periodically as it grows. The lobster is not good to eat immediately after moulting a shell as it absorbs a large amount of water to help it fit into its new shell; the flesh is therefore watery and tasteless. A more mature shell will be thick and encrusted and the creature will feel heavy for its size.

The female lobster has the more tender flesh. The coral-coloured roe under its tail can be cooked separately and used to make lobster butter or added to sauces to impart a delicate flavour.

Buying and Storing

Lobsters are available live or cooked. Live lobsters should be active, with limbs intact. Do not buy a dead uncooked lobster, unless you are certain it has just been killed, as it deteriorates quickly.

When buying cooked lobsters look for limbs intact and bright eyes. They should be heavy for their size and there should be no discoloration at the joints.

Store live lobsters in a damp hessian bag for up to 24 hours until required. Wrap cooked lobster in foil and store in the refrigerator for up to 2 days.

Preparation

Live lobsters are normally sold with their claws banded. If not, secure the large claws with rubber bands. Put lobsters, head down, in a large pan of fast boiling well-salted water or court bouillon (see page 24).

Cover and bring to the boil, then simmer, allowing 12 minutes for a 500 g (1 lb) lobster; 20 minutes for a 1 kg (2 lb) one. For larger lobsters, allow an extra 5 minutes for every additional 500 g (1 lb).

In recipes where a live lobster is not boiled first but grilled, ensure the claws are held with rubber bands. Hold underside down on a board, then place the point of a strong knife on the shell in the centre of the cross-shaped mark between the eyes and plunge it quickly down through the body.

To split a freshly killed lobster for grilling or lobster thermidor, using a sharp knife, cut firmly from the upper body down towards the tail, splitting the tail in two. Save the coral, if any, and the yellow-green liver, which is delicious added to sauces. Discard the gravel sac near the head and the intestine, which is the dark thread-like membrane running down the body.

To grill, use a sharp knife to slit the underside several times to help heat penetration. Brush with oil or melted butter and grill for 12-15 minutes, turning once.

A cooked lobster is split and prepared in the same way. To extract the meat, snap off legs and break each apart at the joint. Remove flesh with a skewer. Snap each claw free near the body, then crack the claw shells with a mallet or a lobster cracker; remove meat in one piece if possible With lobster on its back, cut down either side of the shell, then pull away the bony covering which protects the underside. Starting at the tail end, remove the flesh in one piece.

Serving Suggestions

Good quality lobsters are very good freshly boiled, split in half and served with lemon or lime juice and a sprinkling of pepper. Sauces that go well with lobster include mayonnaise, plain or flavoured with herbs, paprika or garlic; hollandaise; thick sour cream and dill; or tomato and wine. A butter sauce flavoured with the mashed coral is an excellent accompaniment for grilled lobster.

European lobster (uncooked)

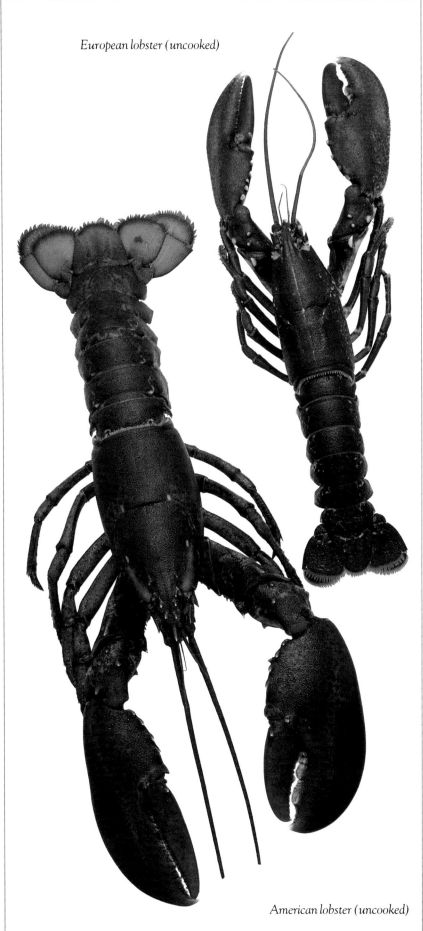

American lobster (uncooked)

American lobster (cooked)

European lobster (cooked)

Spiny lobster tail (cooked)

Spiny lobster tail (uncooked)

Spiny Lobster

The main difference between the spiny lobster and the true lobster is that the spiny lobster (*Palinuras elephas*, var. *vulgaris*) does not have the huge claws of the true lobster. The flesh is comparable in quality and they lend themselves to the same dishes. The smaller the species, the more tender the flesh. They reach a maximum length of 50 cm (20 in) but can be much smaller.

Spiny lobsters are found around the waters of Britain and the Mediterranean. They are reddish-brown with yellow and white markings. Spiny lobsters around European waters are becoming a rare catch, so prices are high when they are available.

Australian marine crayfish are strictly speaking spiny lobsters. Fishing for them in the waters of Southern Australia is a thriving industry. Most are exported to the United States; because of American marketing laws they are called rock lobsters (*Panulirus* and *Jasus*).

To confuse matters further, the spiny lobster is often referred to as crawfish or crayfish, although it should be termed saltwater crayfish, as it is quite different from the small freshwater crayfish (see page 46).

The Western rock lobster (*Panulirus cygnus*) varies in colour from pink to reddish brown and maroon. It is found in Western Australia and is excellent quality.

The Southern rock lobster (*Jasus novaelollandiae*) is yellow, orange or purple, while the Eastern rock lobster (*Jasus verreauxii*) is olive green.

Buying and Storing
Whole spiny lobsters are available live or cooked. These lobsters are however more commonly sold as lobster tails – uncooked or cooked.

When buying live, spiny lobsters should have all their limbs and be active. Do not buy a dead uncooked whole spiny lobster, as the flesh deteriorates quickly.

When buying cooked whole spiny lobsters, again the limbs should be intact, the eyes bright and there should be no discoloration at the joints. The crustacean should be heavy in weight in proportion to its size.

Store live spiny lobsters in a damp hessian bag for up to 24 hours. Wrap cooked ones in foil and store in the refrigerator for up to 2 days.

Spiny lobster (cooked)

Preparation

Put live spiny lobsters in a large pan of cold water, bring slowly to the boil, then boil for 8 minutes per 500 g (1 lb).

To grill uncooked tails, slit the underside of the tail a couple of times to allow for heat penetration, then brush with oil or butter and grill for 5-8 minutes on each side.

To remove the meat from a whole spiny lobster, first break off the claws and legs. Crack the large claws with a lobster cracker or mallet and remove the meat with a skewer.

Twist off the head from the tail. Use kitchen scissors to cut away the thin underside of the tail shell. Gently pull the meat out. Cut along the back of the meat to a depth of 5 mm (¼ in) and discard the dark vein. Reserve the red coral, if any, to make lobster butter or to add flavour to a savoury sauce. Add the greenish liver to the lobster meat.

Lift out the bony portion from the head shell and pick out any further pieces of coral or liver. Use a lobster pick or the point of a knife to pick the meat from the head. Discard the stomach sac and greyish spongy gills from the top of the head.

Break the bony portion into several pieces and remove the meat with a pick or fork.

Serving Suggestions

Serve warm spiny lobster tails plain with a little lime or lemon juice; with mayonnaise, thick sour cream and herbs; or a rich wine and tomato sauce.

To serve in the half shell, lay the cooked spiny lobster on its back and, using a sharp knife, split from the centre to the end of the tail, then from the centre to the head. Cut through the flesh and split open. Wash thoroughly, discarding inedible parts described above.

Flat Lobster

The flat or slipper lobster (*Scyllarus arctus*) has a flat slipper-shaped shell and no claws. It is a small lobster found in the Mediterranean which grows to a maximum length of 13 cm (5 in). The tail meat of the flat lobster has a good flavour but unfortunately there is not much of it, so this crustacean is more often than not relegated to the soup pot.

A larger related species of slipper lobster (*Scyllarides squammosis*) is found off the coast of southern Queensland in Australia and makes good eating. The American species is rarely eaten.

Sand Lobster & Bay Bug

Sand lobsters and bay bugs are small lobster-like crustaceans which have similar quality meat. These include the shovel-nosed lobster (*Scyllaridae*), also called sand lobster or bay lobster, and bay bugs which have no claws, a flattened body and broad antennae. Sand lobsters are sometimes called rudder-nosed lobsters because of their ability to flip backwards and steer themselves with their antennae. They are similar to flat or slipper lobsters and both species make cricket-like noises in the water.

The Moreton Bay bug (*Thenus orientalis*) and Balmain bug (*Ibacus*) are species of sand lobster caught commercially in the coastal waters and bays of south-eastern Australia.

Sand lobster tails (uncooked)

Rock lobster tails (uncooked)

Bay bugs (cooked)

Flat (or Slipper) lobster tails (cooked)

Crab

Crabs are available all year round, but are at their best during the summer. They are one of the choicest shellfish and are readily available either live or cooked. Most crabs are encased in a hard, rigid shell which must be shed at intervals to allow growth. In the first year of a crab's life moulting is very frequent, but after that growth slows down. In Britain it is illegal to sell crabs that are not fully grown – less than 13 cm (5 in) across – or if they are females carrying eggs.

The common crab (*Cancer pagurus*) is a large crab – up to 20 cm (8 in) across – found in Britain and Europe. It is found as far north as Norway, but does not occur on the American side of the Atlantic.

The rock crab (*Cancer irroratus*) has a yellowish back dotted with brown or purple spots, measuring up to 10 cm (4 in). It is found from Labrador to Florida and is a close relative to the Jonah crab (*Cancer borealis*). The Jonah crab has a brick red shell and is a little larger, weighing about 500 g (1 lb). These crabs do not have the fine flavour of many others but are well worth eating.

The blue crab (*Callimectes sapidus*), also known as blue manna or sand crab, is a soft-shell crab with mottled blue body and legs. It is mainly found in North American waters, but has been introduced to the eastern Mediterranean where it has colonized. It is very popular in America and fishing for it extends from Delaware Bay to Florida and the Gulf States. Chesapeake Bay has the biggest catch, around 200 million per year, which is enough to meet the demands of the whole nation. An agile and fast swimming crab, it is caught in baited crab traps in bays and harbours.

An excellent quality crab, the meat at the base of the legs and in the long claws is finely textured and very sweet – it is considered by many to be the finest of all crab meats. They are marketed according to size: whales or slabs are the biggest, at over 13 cm (5 in) across, then come jumbos, primes, hotels and mediums, which are the smallest.

The mud crab (*Scylla serrata*), also known as mangrove crab, is found throughout south-east Asia where it lives in shallow muddy water among the mangroves in creeks and estuaries. Mud crabs are also found around the northern Australian coast, from Western Australia to central New South Wales.

Mud crabs are dull green, grow to about 2 kg (4 lb) and are usually sold live. The flesh in the claws is the most prized as it is sweet and succulent. The body meat has a good flavour, but is coarser.

The Southern stone crab (*Menippe mercenaria*) is caught from the Gulf of Texas round Florida up to the Carolinas, but is regarded by many as belonging to Florida. It lives in deep holes in mud or heaps of rock in tidal creeks and estuaries. It is greyish in colour and has huge claws, one larger than the other. Its four pairs of feet have hairy spiked ends. It has a very hard shell and only the claw meat is edible. Stone crab claws are often available; they are most attractive.

The small shore or green swimming crab (*Carcinus maenus*) is cultivated in the lagoon of Venice. The meat is not particularly highly flavoured and is mainly used for soups and stocks. The shell is green and its maximum width is 7 cm (2½ in). The latin name *maenus* means frenzied, which describes the way the creature fights back when captured. If they are collected after they have shed their old shells but before their new ones have hardened, they can be cooked and eaten whole; such crabs are known as *moleche* in Venice, where they are eaten with great enjoyment.

The spider crab (*Maia squinado*) is so called because of its round body and spider-like legs. It is found in many waters, particularly around the Adriatic. The shell is spiny – hence its other name spiny crab – and ranges in colour from reddish orange to brown. It hides very successfully in rocks, using seaweed and shore plants to disguise itself.

Common crab-underside (cooked)

Common crab (cooked)

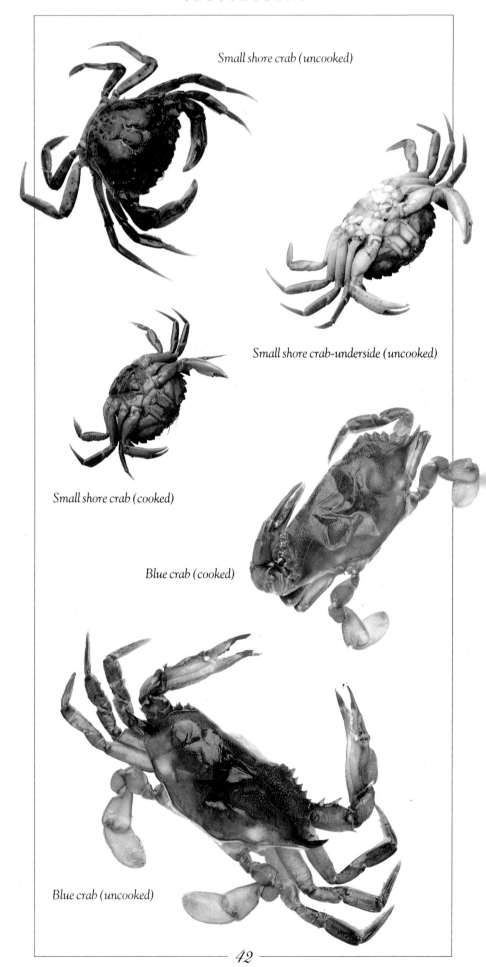

Small shore crab (uncooked)

Small shore crab-underside (uncooked)

Small shore crab (cooked)

Blue crab (cooked)

Blue crab (uncooked)

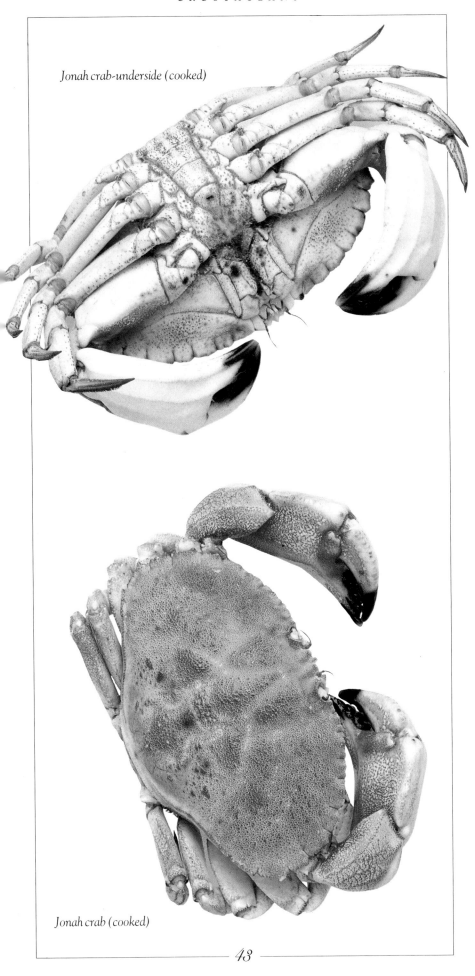

Jonah crab-underside (cooked)

Jonah crab (cooked)

The spider crab has a good flavour and is usually poached and served in its shell.

The red crab (*Geryon quinquedens*) is bright red and up to 15 cm (6 in) across. It is a deep sea crab, found at depths of between 300-900 metres in seas from Nova Scotia to Cuba. It has a good flavour and although the legs are thin, the meat is easily removed.

The snow crab or queen crab (*Chionoecetes opilio*) is found only in cold northerly waters; it is particularly popular in Canada. The claws of the snow crab are long and thin, yielding excellent meat.

The spanner crab (*Ranina ranina*), also known as frog crab, has claws that resemble spanners; the shape also appears frog-like. It is found in the sheltered bays and coastal waters of Australia along southern Queensland and northern New South Wales. It is deep red with cream to pale pink tonings, and grows to over 20 cm (8 in) in length. The meat is white and fine textured. The crabs are usually sold cooked and are best cut lengthwise before extracting the meat.

Buying and Storing

Crabs are usually sold ready cooked. Choose one which has all the limbs intact and feels heavy for its size. Lift the crab and shake before buying – there should be no sound of water.

Uncooked crabs are best bought live as the meat deteriorates quickly once the creature is dead; look for lively, clean-looking crabs.

Store live crabs in a damp hessian bag and eat within 24 hours. Wrap cooked crabs in foil and store in the refrigerator for 1-2 days. Freeze for up to 3 months.

Preparation

If you buy a live crab, kill it humanely before cooking. Place the crab on its back and use an awl to stab the ventral nerve centre under the tail flap, and the point just above the brain between the eyes. Insert the awl several times into each of these points, varying the angle slightly each time. Rinse the crab thoroughly under cold running water to clean.

Place the crab in a pan of cold salted water. Cover and bring slowly to the boil, then boil for 8-10 minutes per 500 g (1 lb), taking care not to overcook. Leave to cool in the water to help keep the flesh tender and moist.

To extract the meat from a cooked crab, place shell down on a work surface. Twist off the claws and legs. Crack the claws with a mallet to extract the meat. Break apart the legs and remove the meat with a skewer.

Twist the bony tail flap free on the underside of the crab and discard. Insert a strong knife between the main shell and underside part where the legs were attached. Prise upwards to detach the underside; set aside.

Scoop out the meat from the main shell, discarding the small greyish-white stomach sac and its appendages, just behind the crab's mouth. Pull away the soft grey feathered gills, known as 'dead men's fingers', along the edges of the underside and discard. Using a heavy knife, split the underside down the middle, then remove the flesh from the crevices using a skewer.

If the crab is to be served in its shell, break away the shell edge along the natural dark rim; scrub the shell thoroughly.

Serving Suggestions

A good quality crab is excellent eaten freshly boiled with lemon and black pepper, or cold with mayonnaise. For a dressed crab, the brown meat from the body is arranged in the centre of the cleaned shell, with the white meat from the claws and legs on either side.

Crab can also be used in countless other dishes: try it grilled (see page 99); combined with vegetables and fruit, such as asparagus (see page 97) or orange (see page 96), to make a tasty salad; as a delicate mousse (see page 98); or as a stuffing for cannelloni or ravioli (see page 100). The meat is sweet and succulent and should not be masked with too many other flavours.

Lesser quality crabs are used as a base for soups and stews, or used in crab cakes, sauces and stuffings.

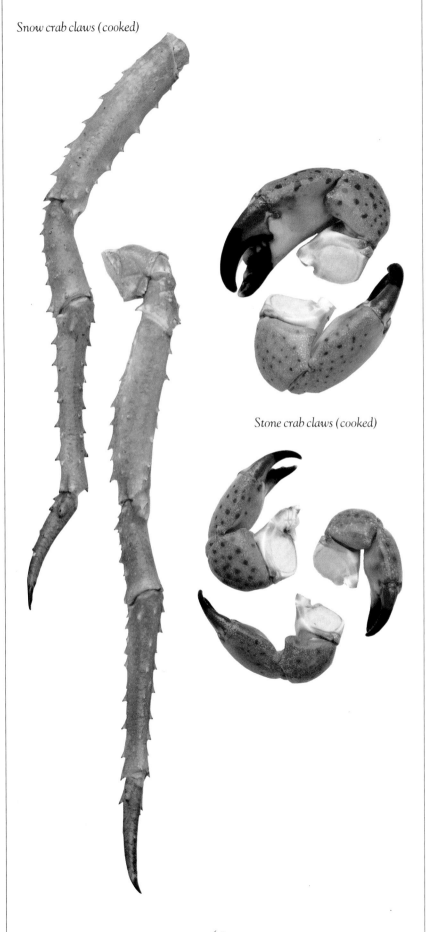

Snow crab claws (cooked)

Stone crab claws (cooked)

Freshwater Crayfish

Freshwater crayfish (*Austropota-mobius pallipes*) are prized for their delicate flavour and are well worth eating when available. In Britain and Europe they tend to be small – about the same size as a Dublin Bay prawn – but much larger species are found in Australia. The Tasmanian crayfish (*Astacopsis gouldi*) for example can reach 6 kg (12 lb).

Murray River crayfish (*Euastacus armatus*) grow to around 2 kg (4 lb) and have spiny blue shells. The similar sized marron (*Cherax tenuimanus*), which comes from freshwater pools around Western Australia, is much favoured for its excellent eating qualities.

The smaller crayfish of Australia, called freshwater yabbies (*Cherax destructor*), are found in rivers, creeks, lakes, dams and billabongs. They are usually brown, but can be green, blue or purple. They are a little larger than the European freshwater crayfish, reaching up to 30.5 cm (12 in) in length.

Buying and Storing
Freshwater crayfish can be bought live or cooked. Check that the claws are intact, the shell firm and that they have a pleasant sea smell. Live crayfish should be lively and intact.

Store live crayfish for up to 24 hours in a damp hessian bag. Wrap cooked crayfish in foil and store in the refrigerator for up to 2 days.

Preparation
Put live crayfish in a large pan of cold water and bring to the boil. Simmer for about 5 minutes, until they turn pinky-red all over. Drain and leave until cool enough to handle. To shell crayfish, twist off the head and peel away the shell from the tail.

Serving Suggestions
Freshwater crayfish are a great delicacy and excellent for starters and seafood platters. They look extremely attractive as the central part of a dish or as a garnish. They can form the focal point of a mixed seafood salad on a bed of interesting leaves, or make a spectacular garnish in their shell beside a plate of poached fish in a creamy sauce. Turbot, salmon and monkfish go very well with crayfish.

Cooked crayfish tails can be simply served on a bed of lettuce with mayonnaise or a vinaigrette dressing.

The cooked shells can be pounded or puréed and used as the basis for a delicious rich sauce to accompany the crayfish tails.

Goose-Necked Barnacle

This creature is quite unlike any other crustacean both in appearance and taste. It consists of a finger-thick tube with a dark dry papery skin covered in tiny scales. On top of this is a pair of white hoof-like pads and between these the creature's feet are visible. This unusual crustacean can be up to 15 cm (6 in) in length.

Goose-necked barnacles (*Polli-cipes cornucopia*) are to be found clinging to rocks in groups. They are very popular in Spain and Portugal but as demand is greater than supply their availability is diminishing.

The edible part is inside the tube; to reach it, pinch the outer skin near the hoof-like pads and prize it off with the fingers. The stalk-like inside is entirely edible, either raw or lightly cooked in salted water.

Crayfish (uncooked)

Crayfish (cooked)

Crayfish tails (cooked)

Squid

Cephalopods

Squid, cuttlefish and octopus are the most well known members of the cephalopod family. They look like translucent bags with heads attached and tentacles. They are strictly speaking molluscs – it is thought they originally had an external shell – but as their methods of cooking and preparation are so different to other molluscs, they warrant their own section. Cephalopods are very good to eat, but need careful preparation and cooking to realize their full potential.

Cephalopod means head-footed, presumably because the tentacles emerge from the head. Cuttlefish and squid have ten tentacles and the octopus has eight. They have no true skeleton, although the cuttlefish and squid have an internal bone. In squid this is transparent and quill-like, but the cuttlefish bone is more substantial; it is dried and used as a lime source for caged birds.

The octopus is the largest of the cephalopods and has two protruding eyes and suckers all along the tentacles. The octopus can change its colour and shape at high speed in order to deter predators.

Another protection all cephalopods have is a sac of dark brown or black ink in the body cavity, which the creature can squirt out to form a protective screen while making its escape.

Cephalopods can be caught in nets or traps; the octopus is some-times speared. However, most of those sold commercially are caught as a by-product of trawling. In Mediterranean countries cephalopods are much appreciated and they are prepared and cooked with great skill. Not so long ago, however, squid was thought to be fit only for bait. Cuttlefish, usually smaller than squid, have a delicate flavour prized in Japanese cooking.

Cephalopods have firm, rather spicy flesh. Octopus needs to be tenderized either by long slow cooking or, for large specimens, by pounding. Smaller octopus can be sliced and shallow- or deep-fried. Squid and cuttlefish are more tender and can be cut up and fried or stewed, or their bodies can be stuffed and braised or baked. Small cuttlefish are very good simply cleaned and fried whole.

Once you are familiar with the parts of the cephalopods, their preparation is relatively simple. However, they are often sold ready cleaned by the fishmonger. The tentacles and fleshy body sac are the only edible parts; the rest is discarded, including the quill-shaped transparent bone of the squid and the white hard cuttlebone of the cuttlefish. The eyes, skin and mouth are also discarded. If the ink sac is to be used in cooking it must be removed from the body intact. The body of the squid and larger cuttlefish is skinned, but the skin of the octopus is not removable.

Selection of cephalopods: sea urchins and squid

Squid

The squid (*Loligo vulgaris*) a long cylindrical body with fins on either side. The head has large eyes and two tentacles, and eight 'arms' surround the parrot-like beak. Squid are much smaller than octopus, reaching a maximum size of 51 cm (20 in). Internally they have a pen-shaped quill, loosely attached to the pouch.

Squid swim strongly near the surface of the water by jet propulsion through their funnels and are very graceful to see; the fins are used for steering. They are almost transparent in the water, making them almost invisible to predators. Like other cephalopods, squid possess sophisticated pigment cells which enable them to change colour rapidly. This explains why some have a mottled purplish-brown skin.

Squid are caught by trawling and are fished thoughout the world, but particularly around the coasts of Europe. The above species is the one fished around the Mediterranean. A slightly larger species (*Loligo forbesi*) is found in the Atlantic as far south as Britain. Another common American species is *Loligo pealei*. All of these squid are similar in appearance.

Their relative, the flying squid (*Todarodes sagittatus*), is rather different. It can be up to twice the size and has a purple hue. The flying squid has flat broad swimming fins to the rear of its body, eight 'arms' and two much longer tentacles. It does not really fly, but can propel itself out of the water and glide above the surface. It needs long slow cooking to tenderize it.

Buying and Storing
When buying whole squid look for those with firm flesh; the head and tentacles should be intact. Squid should have a pleasant sea smell. If the skin is difficult to remove, it is a sign of staleness.

Squid are often sold ready cleaned, either in tubes or sliced into rings. The flesh should be white, without any brown markings.

Preparation
First rinse thoroughly. To prepare squid, hold the head just below the eyes and gently pull away from the body pouch; the soft innards, including the ink sac, will come with it. Discard the innards of the pouch, carefully retaining the ink sac intact if required. Pull back the rim of the body pouch to find the quill-shaped pen. Carefully pull it free and discard.

Cut the head from the tentacles just below the eyes; discard the head. Cut out the small round cartilage at the base of the tentacles.

The tentacles will be in one piece. In the centre is the beak-like mouth, which should be removed by squeezing with the fingers.

Slip your fingers under the skin of the body pouch and peel off, then cut the edible fins from the body. Rinse the squid thoroughly under running cold water.

Serving Suggestions
Squid are most commonly served deep-fried in rings. To deep-fry, coat the rings in egg and breadcrumbs or batter and deep-fry in hot oil for 1-2 minutes; serve with a dipping sauce.

Try the body stuffed and baked (see page 106), or sliced with the tentacles and casseroled in a rich tomato sauce (see pages 104 and 105). In the Mediterranean, squid are often stewed in their own ink with tomatoes, garlic and onions for flavour.

Thinly-sliced squid rings can also be stir-fried quickly with sliced vegetables, or stewed and added to seafood salads.

Large squid are usually sliced before they are fried, casseroled, or stuffed and baked. Small squid are tender enough to be cooked whole; try frying them in oil or butter, adding garlic or herbs to flavour.

Common squid (large and small)

Octopus

The octopus (*Octopus vulgaris*) has a large head with two protruding eyes and eight tentacles, each carrying a twin row of suckers along their length. The body cavity contains a dark brown ink which the creature can squirt to form a screen. This helps to protect it from predators, such as the conger eel. The octopus can also change its colour like a chameleon to disguise itself when under attack.

The octopus lives in deep waters in the winter months, swimming nearer to land in early spring and spending the summer in inshore waters. It can be caught in traps, nets and by spearing, but usually those sold in markets are caught by trawling.

An octopus can reach a length of 3 m (10 ft), although those normally available for sale are much smaller. Size, however, is no guide to quality – it is the smaller specimens which have the most tender succulent flesh. Larger fish need to be beaten to tenderize them before long slow cooking; it is said they should be beaten one hundred times against a rock!

Two other species worth a mention are the smaller octopus (*Octopus macropus*) and the curled octopus (*Eledone cirrosa*). They are both inferior in quality to the large octopus but can make very good eating if cooked correctly. *Octopus macropus* has a maximum length of 1.2 m (4 ft) with long thin elegant tentacles. It is found in warm waters throughout the world. The curled octopus has a maximum length of 41 cm (16 in) and has curled tentacles each with only a single row of suckers. Both these species are very good cooked in a rich spicy tomato sauce.

Buying and Storing
When buying octopus look for firm resilient flesh with a pleasant sea smell. The larger tougher fish are usually tenderized before being offered for sale. They are also usually sold ready cleaned. If not, clean the octopus yourself (as described below) before storing. Store in a container in the refrigerator for up to 24 hours, or freeze for up to 3 months. Only freeze specimens that you know to be absolutely fresh.

Preparation
To prepare octopus, hold the head firmly and, using a sharp knife, cut through the flesh below the eyes, severing the head from the tentacles. Invert the body pouch and remove the intestines and ink sac. Wash the body pouch well under running cold water. Pick up the tentacles and, with the index finger underneath the centre, push the beak up and cut it away.

To tenderize hood and tentacles, if necessary, beat with a steak mallet until they feel soft and have lost their springiness. Remove any scales which may be left in the suckers. An octopus which is less than 10 cm (4 in) does not need beating to tenderize.

Plunge the octopus into boiling salted water for 5 minutes; drain well and leave until cool enough to handle.

Using a sharp knife or scissors, cut the tentacles into separate pieces and leave whole or chop, according to the recipe.

Serving Suggestions
Octopus needs tenderizing to make it palatable and long slow braising or stewing is probably the best method. However, the flesh of smaller ones will be tender if cooked very briefly: cut into pieces and stir-fry or deep-fry until tender.

Octopus can be used in Mediterranean-style soups; casseroles such as provençal; cooked in wine (see page 109); served in a spicy coconut sauce (see page 110); in a salad with garlic dressing; in deep-fried seafood dishes; or stir-fried with soy sauce and vegetables.

Octopus

Cuttlefish

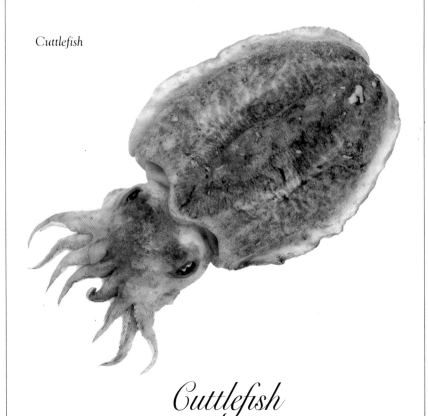

Cuttlefish

The cuttlefish (*Sepia officinalis*) is the smallest member of the cephalopod family. It is oval in shape and can range in length from 2.5-25 cm (1-10 in). The smallest specimens are the sweetest and most tender.

Cuttlefish have eight short tentacles and two much larger ones. The colour varies, but there are often mottled or zebra-like markings on the back. Inside the body there is a hard bone which must be removed. Cuttlefish secrete a dark ink which was formally used to make the colour sepia; the Italian name for the fish is *seppia*. Cuttlefish are fished in the eastern Atlantic, the Mediterranean and off the south coast of Britain.

There is a smaller version called Little Cuttlefish (*Sepiola rondeleti*) which has a maximum length of 4 cm (1½ in). It has two ear-shaped flaps projecting towards the rear of the body and short tentacles. It is usually cleaned and fried whole.

Buying and Storing
Cuttlefish are available whole and should have clean undamaged bodies with a pleasant sea smell. The flesh should be firm and not discoloured. The ink sac is easily broken when it is being caught, but the ink washes off easily.

Cuttlefish should ideally be cooked as soon as possible after purchase. Clean the fish, place in a plastic container and store in the refrigerator for up to 24 hours, or in the freezer for 3 months.

Preparation
To prepare a large cuttlefish, place it bone side down on a board. Slit the mantle with a sharp knife, open out and remove the gut and cuttle bone; discard. The ink sac, if intact, can be used for cooking. Cut the body in half and remove the skin. The tentacles can be eaten, once the beak is removed, but it is the body which is most commonly used.

Slice the body thinly into rings or sections, or leave it whole for stuffing and baking; score it diagonally before cooking. Chop the tentacles.

Small cuttlefish are usually cleaned and served whole. They are best fried, grilled or barbecued.

Small cuttlefish need only brief cooking as they toughen easily, but large fish need longer cooking to tenderize them.

Serving Suggestions

Grill small cuttlefish with a wine and herb marinade; use them in Chinese stir-fry and steamed dishes, flavoured with garlic, ginger and chilli; make criss-cross cuts across the body to absorb the flavours and cook them in spicy or curry sauces.

Use larger cuttlefish sliced in casseroles or cooked in a sauce – they are particularly good in rich tomato or wine sauces; dip strips or rings in batter and deep-fry; or stuff the body and bake.

Sea Urchin

The sea urchin (*Strongylocentus droebachiensis*) is particularly popular in France and other Mediterranean countries, where they are displayed to great effect in large baskets, in the coastal towns where they are harvested. The edible parts are the star-shaped ovaries, revealed when the creature is cut open.

The sea urchin gets its name from the old English name for urchin: hedgehog. It reaches up to 8 cm (3 in) in diameter and is caught off the coasts of the Mediterranean; it is also common on the south and west coasts of Ireland.

Buying and Storing

·Sea urchins are not generally marketed but are often sold from the beaches and harbours where they are landed. The inside should be fresh and glistening and they should be consumed as soon as possible. They are always sold live as they deteriorate quickly.

Preparation

Cut the sea urchin open horizontally across the middle with scissors, or a special tool called a *coupe-oursin*. The edible parts are the fine orange or pink ovaries which can be clearly seen inside.

Serving Suggestions

The small ovaries are eaten from the shell, sprinkled with a little lemon juice. They can also be added to omelettes and scrambled eggs, made into a sauce for poached fish, or used to garnish seafood dishes.

Sea urchin (green)

Sea urchin (purple), cut to reveal edible ovaries

Sea urchin (yellow)

Clam Fritters

2 kg (4 lb) small clams in shell
125 ml (4 fl oz/½ cup) dry white wine
1 bay leaf
1 sprig of thyme
vegetable oil for deep-frying
BATTER:
125 g (4 oz) plain flour
salt and pepper, to taste
½ teaspoon paprika
2 eggs, beaten
250 ml (8 fl oz/1 cup) milk
TO SERVE:
1 tablespoon grated Parmesan cheese

1 Scrub clams thoroughly under running cold water, scraping off any barnacles. Discard any that are cracked or not tightly closed. Put in a large saucepan with wine, bay leaf and thyme. Cover tightly and steam for about 5 minutes, until shells have opened. Drain, discarding any clams that have not opened. Remove clams from shells and chop finely.

2 Sift flour, salt, pepper and paprika into a bowl. Make a well in the centre and add eggs. Beat in milk a little at a time until a smooth batter is formed. Stir in clams.

3 In a deep-fryer, heat oil to 180C (350F) or until a cube of bread browns in 30 seconds. Add dessertspoons of clam mixture, a few at a time, and deep-fry for 2-3 minutes, until puffy and golden brown. Drain well on absorbent kitchen paper. Sprinkle with Parmesan cheese and serve with salad, as a light meal or starter.

Serves 4.

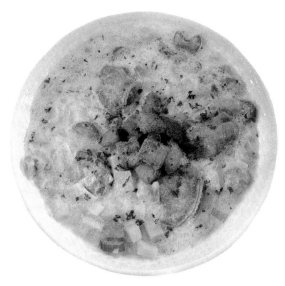

Clam Chowder

185 ml (6 fl oz/³⁄₄ cup) dry white wine
1 kg (2 lb) small clams in shell, cleaned
30 g (1 oz) butter
90 g (3 oz) lean bacon, diced
2 leeks, shredded
2 sticks celery, thinly sliced
500 g (1 lb) potatoes, chopped
250 ml (8 fl oz/1 cup) milk
125 ml (4 fl oz/½ cup) double (thick) cream
2 tablespoons chopped parsley
salt and pepper, to taste
TO SERVE:
garlic croûtons (see below)

1 Put wine and 250 ml (8 fl oz/ 1 cup) water in a large saucepan. Add clams, cover tightly and cook over a high heat for about 3-4 minutes, until shells have opened. Drain, reserving liquid; discard any clams that have not opened. Remove clams from shells and set aside.

2 In a large saucepan, melt butter, add bacon and fry until lightly coloured. Add leeks and celery and fry for 5 minutes. Add potatoes and strain clam cooking liquid into pan. Bring to the boil, cover and simmer for about 20 minutes, until potatoes are tender.

3 Add milk, cream, parsley, clams, salt and pepper and simmer for 5 minutes. Serve with garlic croûtons, as a light meal.

Serves 4.

Garlic croûtons: Fry 1 cm (½ in) cubes of crustless white bread in hot oil flavoured with a crushed garlic clove until crisp and golden. Drain on absorbent kitchen paper.

Pasta with Clam Sauce

1 red pepper
250 g (8 oz/2 cups) strong white flour
pinch of salt
2 eggs, beaten
1 tablespoon olive oil
SAUCE:
60 g (2 oz) unsalted butter
1 onion, finely chopped
397 g (14 oz) can chopped tomatoes
pinch of sugar
salt and pepper, to taste
500 g (1 lb) clams in shell, cooked
2 teaspoons chopped tarragon
3 tablespoons chopped parsley

1 Grill red pepper until evenly charred. Wrap in foil until cool, then remove skin and discard seeds. Purée in a blender or food processor.

Sift flour and salt onto a work surface. Make a well in the centre, add eggs, oil and red pepper purée, then gradually mix in flour to form a soft dough.

2 Put the dough through the fine setting of a pasta machine; or roll out as thinly as possible, then roll up like a Swiss roll and cut into strips; set aside.

To make sauce, in a pan, melt butter, add onion and fry until softened. Add tomatoes, sugar, salt and pepper and simmer for 20 minutes. Purée in a blender or food processor and return to pan.

3 Remove clams from shells and add to sauce with herbs; warm through briefly.

Cook pasta in plenty of boiling salted water for 3-4 minutes; drain well. Serve the pasta topped with the sauce.

Serves 4.

Note: Use a ready-made fresh pasta, flavoured with tomato, if preferred.

Variation: Replace the clams with mussels.

Clam Salad with Chilli Dressing

750 g (1 ½ lb) clams in shell, cleaned
salt and pepper, to taste
125 g (4 oz) fine green beans
125 g (4 oz) button mushrooms
60 g (2 oz/½ cup) pine nuts
salad leaves (eg young spinach, rocket, lettuce)
CHILLI DRESSING:
1 red chilli
½ teaspoon fennel seeds
1 tablespoon lemon juice
60 ml (2 fl oz/¼ cup) virgin olive oil
TO GARNISH:
sprigs of chervil

1 Put clams in a saucepan with a little water, salt and pepper. Cover tightly and shake pan over high heat for 2-3 minutes, until the shells have opened. Drain and discard any clams that have not opened. Remove clams from shells.

2 To make dressing, wearing rubber gloves, remove stalk from chilli, halve lengthwise and scrape out seeds; finely chop flesh. Crush fennel seeds and put in a small bowl with chilli, lemon juice, oil, salt and pepper. Whisk until thickened.

Blanch beans in boiling salted water for 2 minutes; drain and refresh under running cold water.

3 Thinly slice mushrooms. Lightly toast pine nuts. Arrange salad leaves on 4 individual serving plates. Sprinkle with beans, mushrooms and clams. Drizzle over the dressing and sprinkle with pine nuts. Garnish with chervil and serve as a light lunch or starter.

Serves 4.

Variation: Replace clams with mussels.

Mussel Soufflés

750 g (1½ lb) mussels in shell
185 ml (6 fl oz/¾ cup) dry white wine
1 clove garlic, crushed
few strands of saffron
few sprigs of parsley
1 bay leaf
salt and pepper, to taste
30 g (1 oz) butter
2 teaspoons plain flour
1 tablespoon lemon juice
2 eggs, separated
30 g (1 oz/¼ cup) grated Gruyère cheese
1 tablespoon grated Parmesan cheese

1 Preheat oven to 180C (350F/Gas 4). Scrub mussels thoroughly under running cold water. Scrape off any barnacles and pull off the beard which protrudes between the shells. Discard any that are open or cracked. Rinse the mussels in a colander.

Put mussels and wine in a saucepan, cover and cook over a high heat, shaking pan, for about 3 minutes, until shells have opened. Strain, reserving cooking liquid; discard any mussels that have not opened. Remove mussels from shells and set aside.

2 Put cooking liquid, garlic, saffron, parsley, bay leaf, salt and pepper in a pan; boil until reduced to 185 ml (6 fl oz/¾ cup); strain into a jug. In the same pan, melt butter, add flour and cook for 1 minute. Add strained cooking liquid and cook, stirring, until thickened and smooth; stir in lemon juice. Remove from heat and stir in egg yolks and cheeses. In a bowl, whisk egg whites until stiff; fold into sauce. Check seasoning.

3 Divide mussels between 4 buttered ramekin dishes. Spoon soufflé mixture on top and bake in the oven for 20 minutes, until risen and golden brown. Serve immediately, as a light lunch or starter.

Serves 4.

Mussels with Two Sauces

2 kg (4 lb) mussels in shell, cleaned
125 ml (4 fl oz/½ cup) dry white wine
TOMATO BASIL SAUCE:
397 g (14 oz) can chopped tomatoes
1 tablespoon tomato purée (paste)
2 teaspoons torn basil leaves
1 teaspoon chopped oregano
pinch of sugar
salt and pepper, to taste
FENNEL SAUCE:
30 g (1 oz) butter
1 leek, finely chopped
1 fennel bulb, finely chopped
60 ml (2 fl oz/¼ cup) double (thick) cream

1 Put mussels and wine in a large saucepan, cover and cook over a high heat, shaking pan, for 4-6 minutes, until shells have opened. Drain, discarding any mussels that have not opened; discard the empty half shells. Arrange mussels in their half shells on an ovenproof dish and keep warm.
2 To make tomato basil sauce, put all the ingredients in a saucepan and simmer for 15 minutes, until thickened and smooth.

To make fennel sauce, in a pan melt butter, add leek and fennel, cover and cook for about 5 minutes, until softened. Add cream, season to taste and simmer for 2 minutes. Purée in a blender or food processor.
3 Arrange mussels on individual serving plates and fill shells alternately with the two sauces. Serve as a starter or light lunch.

Serves 4-6.

Mussels with Pesto

2 kg (4 lb) mussels in shell, cleaned
125 ml (4 fl oz/½ cup) dry white wine
PESTO:
60 g (2 oz) basil leaves
2 cloves garlic
30 g (1 oz/¼ cup) pine nuts
salt and pepper, to taste
30 g (1 oz/¼ cup) grated Parmesan cheese
4 tablespoons olive oil
TO FINISH:
30 g (1 oz/¼ cup) dry breadcrumbs

1 Preheat oven to 200C (400F/Gas 6). Put mussels and wine in a large saucepan, cover and cook over a high heat, shaking pan, for 4-6 minutes, until shells have opened. Drain, discarding any mussels that have not opened; discard the empty half shells. Set mussels aside.

2 To make pesto, put basil, garlic, pine nuts, salt and pepper in a mortar, and pound until well blended. (This can alternatively be done in a food processor.) Blend in cheese, then add oil a little at a time, until the consistency is thick and creamy.

3 Arrange mussels in their half shells in 4 shallow ovenproof dishes. Spread a little pesto over each and sprinkle with breadcrumbs. Bake in the oven for 10 minutes, until piping hot. Serve immediately, as a starter.

Serves 4-6.

Garlic Mussel Puffs

1 kg (2 lb) mussels in shell, cleaned
125 ml (4 fl oz/½ cup) dry white wine
2 tablespoons thick sour cream
1 clove garlic, crushed
1 tablespoon chopped parsley
1 tablespoon snipped chives
30 g (1 oz/¼ cup) grated Gruyère cheese
salt and pepper, to taste
250 g (8 oz) packet puff pastry
beaten egg, to glaze

1 Preheat oven to 220C (425F/Gas 7). Put mussels and wine in a large saucepan, cover and cook over a high heat, shaking pan, for 3-4 minutes, until shells have opened; drain, discarding any mussels that have not opened. Remove mussels from shells.

2 Mix together thick sour cream, garlic, herbs, cheese, salt and pepper. Add mussels and mix well. On a lightly floured surface, roll out pastry thinly and cut out about forty 5 cm (2 in) rounds. Put a mussel and a little sauce on each round, dampen pastry edges and fold in half, sealing well.

3 Place the puffs on a dampened baking sheet and brush with beaten egg. Bake in the oven for about 10 minutes, until puffed up and golden brown. Serve piping hot, as a starter or snack.

Serves 6-8.

Variation: Replace mussels with small clams.

Mussels in Wine & Cream Sauce

500 ml (16 fl oz/2 cups) Muscadet wine
bouquet garni
3 kg (6 lb) mussels in shell, cleaned
30 g (1 oz) butter
2 shallots, finely chopped
pinch of turmeric
125 ml (4 fl oz/½ cup) double (thick) cream
2 egg yolks
salt and pepper, to taste
dash of Tabasco sauce
2 teaspoons chopped tarragon

1 Put wine and bouquet garni in a large saucepan. Add mussels, cover and cook over a high heat, shaking pan, for 5-6 minutes, until shells open. Remove mussels with a slotted spoon and discard any that have not opened. Remove mussels from shells and set aside. Boil cooking liquid until reduced by half.
2 In a clean pan, melt butter, add shallots and fry gently until softened. Stir in reduced liquid and boil until reduced again by one third. Strain and return to pan with turmeric and all but 1 tablespoon cream; simmer for 1 minute.
3 Blend egg yolks with remaining cream and whisk in a little of the hot liquid. Whisk this slowly into pan and heat gently, without boiling, until thickened and smooth. Season with salt, pepper and Tabasco. Add mussels and warm through. Sprinkle with tarragon to serve.

Serves 4.

Oysters Rockefeller

250 g (8 oz) young spinach leaves
125 g (4 oz) bacon, rinds removed
125 g (4 oz) butter
3 spring onions, finely chopped
2 tablespoons chopped celery leaves
2 tablespoons chopped parsley
60 g (2 oz/½ cup) dry breadcrumbs
1 tablespoon grated Parmesan cheese
1 tablespoon Pernod
24 large oysters, cleaned
coarse sea salt

1 Preheat oven to 220C (425F/Gas 7). Cook spinach with just the water clinging to the leaves after washing for 3-4 minutes, until wilted; drain well and chop finely. Grill bacon until crisp, then chop finely. In a saucepan, melt butter, add spring onions, celery leaves, parsley, spinach, bacon, breadcrumbs and cheese; mix well. Stir in Pernod. Set aside.

2 To open each oyster, hold in absorbent kitchen paper on a work surface, flatter shell uppermost and hinged end towards you. Insert the point of an oyster knife into the gap in the hinge linking the shells and twist the blade to snap shells apart.

Slide blade along the inside of the upper shell to sever the muscle. Remove any broken shell from the oyster with the point of the knife. Discard empty half shells.

3 Cover the bases of 4 ovenproof serving plates with sea salt. Set the oysters in their half shells in the salt. Divide prepared stuffing between them and bake in the oven for 6-8 minutes, until bubbling. Serve immediately, as a starter.

Serves 4.

Oysters with Caviar & 'Seaweed'

24 large oysters, cleaned
12 quails' eggs
125 g (4 oz) crème fraîche
1 tablespoon snipped chives
60 g (2 oz) caviar
SEAWEED:
500 g (1 lb) dark cabbage
vegetable oil for deep-frying
1 teaspoon caster sugar
salt, to taste

1 Open oysters and discard flatter top shells. Boil quails' eggs for 1 minute, drain, cool and shell. Mix together crème fraîche and chives.
2 To make 'seaweed', shred cabbage by rolling up leaves tightly and slicing thinly with a sharp knife. Heat oil to 180C (350F). Add a handful of cabbage, taking care as the oil will spit, count to ten, then remove with a slotted spoon. Drain well on absorbent kitchen paper. Repeat with remaining cabbage. Sprinkle with sugar and salt.
3 Arrange 'seaweed' on 4 individual serving plates. Place 6 oysters on each plate. On each shell place a halved quails' egg, a spoonful of crème fraîche and a little caviar. Serve immediately, as a starter.

Serves 4.

Champagne Oysters

48 oysters, cleaned
125 g (4 oz) butter
2 tablespoons finely chopped spring onion
2 teaspoons chopped tarragon
1 teaspoon chopped mint
375 ml (12 fl oz/1½ cups) champagne
salt and pepper, to taste
TO GARNISH:
sprigs of mint

1 To open oysters, hold with absorbent kitchen paper on a work surface, flatter shell uppermost and hinged end towards you. Insert the point of an oyster knife into the gap in the hinge and twist the blade to snap shells apart. Slide blade along the inside of the upper shell to sever the muscle. Discard empty half shells. Remove any broken shell from the oyster with the point of the knife. Remove oysters from shells and set aside. Arrange shells in a circle on 4 individual serving plates.

2 In a saucepan, melt 30 g (1 oz) butter, add spring onion, tarragon and mint and cook for 1 minute. Add champagne and salt and pepper, bring to the boil, then simmer until liquid is reduced by half. Whisk in remaining butter a piece at a time, until sauce is thickened and creamy.

3 Add oysters to sauce and cook gently for 2 minutes. Spoon oysters back into shells, covering each with a little sauce. Garnish with mint and serve with fingers of toast, as a starter.

Serves 4.

Scallops with Saffron Sauce

8 scallops in shell
45 g (1½ oz) butter
1 small onion, finely chopped
2 tablespoons dry vermouth
125 ml (4 fl oz/½ cup) dry white wine
2 tomatoes, skinned, seeded and chopped
¼ teaspoon powdered saffron
125 g (4 oz) fine asparagus tips
3 tablespoons crème fraîche
salt and pepper, to taste

1 First open scallop shells. Holding scallop in a cloth with flat shell uppermost, insert small knife into the small opening between shells. Work blade across inside of flat shell to sever internal muscle. Prise shells apart.

2 Carefully loosen scallops from shells, rinse, removing any dark strands, and pat dry on absorbent kitchen paper.

3 In a frying pan, melt half the butter and quickly fry scallops for 2-3 minutes, until they turn opaque. Remove from pan with any juices and keep warm.

In the same pan, melt remaining butter, add onion and fry for about 5 minutes, until softened. Add vermouth, wine, tomatoes and saffron; bring to the boil, then simmer until liquid has reduced by half.

Meanwhile, lightly steam asparagus for 3-4 minutes; add to pan with scallops, crème fraîche, salt and pepper. Simmer for 2 minutes; check seasoning. Serve with steamed new potatoes or pasta.

Serves 4.

Note: If buying shelled scallops, use 750 g (1½ lb).

Variation: Serve in the cleaned shells, with toast, as a starter for 6-8.

Scallop Mousselines

500 g (1 lb) shelled queen scallops
90 ml (3 fl oz/⅓ cup) dry vermouth
2 tablespoons lemon juice
125 ml (4 fl oz/½ cup) double (thick) cream
2 egg yolks
salt and pepper, to taste
SAUCE:
90 ml (3 fl oz/⅓ cup) dry vermouth
125 ml (4 fl oz/½ cup) double (thick) cream
30 g (1 oz) unsalted butter
2 teaspoons chopped tarragon
pinch of paprika

1 Preheat oven to 180C (350F/Gas 4). Rinse scallops, removing any dark strands, and pat dry with absorbent kitchen paper; remove the corals and set aside. In a large pan, heat vermouth and lemon juice, add scallops and simmer for 1 minute; remove with a slotted spoon, reserving liquid, and put in a blender. Heat cream until luke-warm. Blend scallops until smooth; add reserved cooking liquid, egg yolks and cream; blend for a few seconds. Season with salt and pepper.
2 Divide mixture between 4 buttered ramekin dishes, put in a roasting pan half filled with hot water and bake in the oven for 15-20 minutes, until firm to the touch.
3 Meanwhile, make sauce. Boil vermouth in a small saucepan until reduced by half. Add cream and again reduce by half. Keeping sauce at a simmer, add half the butter in small pieces, season with salt and pepper and stir in tarragon.

In a small pan, melt remaining butter add reserved corals and cook for 1-2 minutes.

Turn the mousselines out onto 4 individual warmed serving plates. Pour over the sauce, sprinkle with paprika and garnish with corals. Serve immediately, as a starter.

Serves 4.

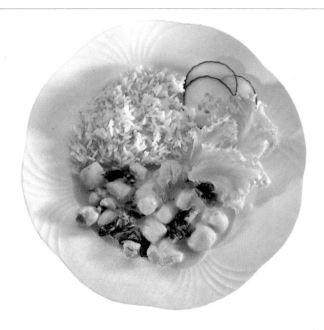

Scallops & Spinach Chardonnay

185 g (6 oz) young spinach leaves
salt, to taste
90 g (3 oz) butter
1 small onion, finely chopped
2 sprigs of parsley
125 ml (4 fl oz/½ cup) white Chardonnay wine
125 ml (4 fl oz/½ cup) fish stock
6 black peppercorns
60 ml (2 fl oz/¼ cup) double (thick) cream
500-750 g (1-1½ lb) shelled queen scallops

1 Put spinach in a pan with just the water clinging to the leaves after washing and add a pinch of salt. Cover and cook for 3-4 minutes, until the leaves have just wilted. Drain and refresh under running cold water. Press out as much water as possible from the leaves. Set aside.
2 In a saucepan, melt 30 g (1 oz) butter, add onion and fry until softened but not coloured. Add parsley, wine, stock and peppercorns. Bring to the boil, then simmer until reduced by two thirds. Strain and return to pan with cream. Keeping sauce at a gentle simmer, add remaining butter a small piece at a time, stirring with each addition, until sauce is smooth and shiny.
3 Rinse scallops, removing any dark strands, and pat dry with absorbent kitchen paper. Add to pan, cover and cook for about 4 minutes, until just cooked. Stir in spinach and heat through. Taste and add salt if necessary. Serve with saffron rice and a crisp salad.

Serves 4.

Poached Scallops in a Nest

125 g (4 oz) fine green beans
4 small carrots
4 small courgettes (zucchini)
500 g (1 lb) shelled queen scallops, cleaned
2 tablespoons lemon juice
6 tablespoons dry white wine
1 teaspoon green peppercorns, lightly crushed
90 g (3 oz) unsalted butter, in pieces
2 teaspoons chopped mint
salt, to taste

1 Cut beans in half lengthwise. Peel carrots, then pare carrots and courgettes (zucchini) into ribbons, using a mandolin or potato peeler; set aside.

Rinse scallops, removing any dark strands, and pat dry with absorbent kitchen paper.

2 Put lemon juice, wine and peppercorns in a saucepan and bring to the boil. Simmer for 3-4 minutes, then add scallops, cover and cook gently for 3-5 minutes, until they feel firm and look opaque. Remove with a slotted spoon and keep warm.

3 Boil the pan juices until reduced to about 1 tablespoon. Over a very low heat, beat in butter a small piece at a time, to form a smooth shiny sauce. Stir in mint and salt and keep warm.

Blanch beans, carrots and courgettes (zucchini) in boiling water for 1 minute; drain and arrange in a 'nest' shape on 4 individual warmed plates. Pile scallops in the centre and pour sauce over the top. Serve immediately.

Serves 4.

Scallops in Tomato Cream

3 ripe tomatoes
500 g (1 lb) shelled queen scallops
1 tablespoon sunflower oil
1 small leek, white part only, finely chopped
4 tablespoons dry vermouth
4 tablespoons dry white wine
155 ml (5 fl oz/⅔ cup) fromage frais
8 basil leaves, torn
salt and pepper, to taste
TO GARNISH:
sprigs of basil

1 Plunge tomatoes into a bowl of boiling water for 1 minute, then remove and peel away skins. Cut in half and squeeze out seeds; finely chop tomato flesh.

Rinse scallops, removing any dark strands and pat dry with absorbent kitchen paper.

2 In a frying pan, heat oil, add leek and fry gently for about 5 minutes, until softened. Add vermouth and wine and bring to the boil, then simmer for 2 minutes. Add scallops, cover and cook for 3-5 minutes, until opaque and firm. Remove with a slotted spoon and keep warm.

3 Boil liquid remaining in pan until reduced to 2 tablespoons. Add tomatoes and heat through. Stir in fromage frais and basil and heat through; do not allow to boil. Season with salt and pepper.

Spoon the sauce onto 4 warmed individual serving plates, pile scallops in the centre and garnish with basil. Serve as a starter or light lunch.

Serves 4.

Spicy Stir-fried Abalone

2 abalone in shell
2 tablespoons sunflower oil
1 clove garlic, chopped
1 teaspoon chopped fresh root (green) ginger
1 dried red chilli
2 tablespoons soy sauce
2 tablespoons rice wine or dry sherry
1 teaspoon sugar
1 teaspoon tomato purée (paste)
1 tablespoon shredded spring onion

1 First shell abalone. Push the tip of an oyster knife (or other strong small knife) into the thin end of the shell underneath the flesh. Work the blade until the muscle is free. Take out the white meat; rinse thoroughly, discarding the intestine; pat dry with absorbent kitchen paper.
2 Cut abalone into very thin slices, then pound with a mallet until limp and velvety to tenderize.
3 In a wok or frying pan, heat oil and briefly fry garlic, ginger and chilli. Add abalone and stir-fry for

30 seconds. Remove abalone with a slotted spoon.

Add soy sauce, rice wine or sherry, sugar and tomato purée (paste) to pan. Bring to the boil, then simmer for 2 minutes. Return abalone to pan and heat through.

Remove chilli and sprinkle with shredded spring onion to serve. Serve as a light lunch.

Serves 4.

Note: If using shelled abalone, you will need 375 g (12 oz) abalone meat.

Spicy Prawns & Chinese Pancakes

315 g (10 oz/2½ cups) plain flour
a little sesame oil
500 g (1 lb) raw king prawns
1 tablespoon groundnut oil
1 teaspoon finely chopped fresh root (green) ginger
2 teaspoons finely chopped spring onion
1 tablespoon rice wine or dry sherry
2 teaspoons soy sauce
½ teaspoon chilli bean sauce
1 teaspoon tomato purée (paste)
2 teaspoons each clear honey and lemon juice
TO SERVE:
hoisin sauce
½ cucumber, cut into sticks
4 spring onions, cut into sticks

1 Sift flour into a bowl. Gradually add 280 ml (9 fl oz/1⅛ cups) very hot water, mixing with a fork or chopsticks to a soft dough. Knead on a lightly floured surface for 5 minutes. Put in a polythene bag and leave for 30 minutes. Knead briefly, then roll into a sausage, 46 cm (18 in) long; cut into 16 pieces.
2 Shape 2 pieces of dough into balls. Dip one ball in sesame oil and place on top of the other. Roll out the 2 balls together to a 15 cm (6 in) round. Repeat with remaining dough. Heat a wok or large non-stick frying pan (without added oil) and cook pancakes until lightly browned, turning once. When cool enough to handle, peel pancakes apart, wrap in foil and keep warm in a steamer.
3 Peel prawns, leaving tail intact, slit down the back and remove dark vein. Heat groundnut oil in wok or frying pan, add ginger and spring onion and stir-fry briefly. Add prawns and stir-fry for 1-2 minutes, until pink. Add remaining ingredients, and simmer for 3 minutes. Turn into a warmed serving dish.

Diners serve themselves: spread pancakes with a little hoisin sauce, top with a prawn and a little cucumber and spring onion, then roll up. Serve as a starter.

Serves 4.

Prawn Satay

750 g (1½ lb) raw king prawns
1 teaspoon turmeric
1 teaspoon ground cumin
½ teaspoon ground fennel
½ teaspoon finely grated lemon rind
1 tablespoon light soft brown sugar
30 g (1 oz) creamed coconut
DIP:
1 red chilli
2 tablespoons clear honey
4 tablespoons cider vinegar
6 thin slices cucumber
TO GARNISH:
sprigs of parsley

1 To peel prawns, break or cut off heads. Slip off tail and shell.
2 Using a small sharp knife, slit down centre back and remove dark intestinal vein.

In a bowl, mix together spices, lemon rind and sugar. Dissolve coconut in 4 tablespoons boiling water and add to bowl. Add prawns and leave to marinate for 1-2 hours, stirring occasionally.

To prepare dip, wearing rubber gloves, cut chilli in half lengthwise, carefully remove and discard seeds. Finely chop chilli and mix with honey and vinegar. Cut cucumber slices into quarters and add to dip. Divide between 4 tiny serving dishes.
3 Thread prawns onto bamboo skewers and cook under a preheated moderate grill for 5-6 minutes, turning occasionally. Arrange on individual serving plates and garnish with parsley. Serve immediately, with the dip, as a starter.

Serves 4.

Singapore Prawn Parcels

1 red chilli
90 g (3 oz) fine green beans
90 g (3 oz) beansprouts
¼ cucumber, chopped
250 g (8 oz) peeled prawns, thawed if frozen
3 tablespoons shredded spring onion
1 tablespoon chopped coriander
1 crisp hearted lettuce
coriander leaves, to garnish
DRESSING:
60 g (2 oz/⅓ cup) shelled peanuts, roasted
1 teaspoon soy sauce
1 clove garlic, crushed
1 teaspoon light soft brown sugar
4 tablespoons orange juice
1 tablespoon lemon juice

1 Wear rubber gloves to prepare chilli: cut in half; carefully discard stalk and seeds; then chop finely. Cut beans into short lengths and blanch in boiling water for 2 minutes. Blanch beansprouts for a few seconds. Drain vegetables and refresh under running cold water. Mix together chilli, beans, beansprouts, cucumber, prawns, spring onion and coriander.
2 To make dressing, in a food processor, roughly grind peanuts, then mix with soy sauce, garlic, sugar, orange and lemon juices. Taste and add salt if necessary. Add to prawn mixture and stir well.
3 Separate lettuce leaves. Place a spoonful of prawn mixture on each leaf. Arrange on a serving platter and garnish with coriander. Serve as a starter.

Serves 6-8.

Prawn & Coconut Fritters

250 g (8 oz) peeled prawns, thawed if frozen
4 spring onions, chopped
60 g (2 oz) creamed coconut, grated
90 g (3 oz) beansprouts, roughly chopped
90 g (3 oz/¾ cup) plain flour
1 teaspoon baking powder
2 cloves garlic, crushed
1 teaspoon chopped fresh root (green) ginger
2 eggs, beaten
1 teaspoon salt, and pepper to taste
1 teaspoon soy sauce
vegetable oil for deep-frying
TO GARNISH:
salad leaves
lime slices
shredded spring onion

1 Put prawns and spring onions in a blender or food processor and work until finely chopped. Dissolve coconut in 2 tablespoons boiling water and add to blender or food processor with remaining ingredients. Process for a few seconds to mix.

2 Heat oil to 180C (350F) or until a little mixture dropped into oil immediately rises to surface. Drop dessertspoons of mixture, a few at a time, into oil and cook for 3-4 minutes, until puffy and golden brown. Remove with a slotted spoon and drain on absorbent kitchen paper. Keep warm while cooking remaining mixture.

3 Arrange salad leaves on individual serving plates. Make a cut through to the centre of each lime slice, then twist. Pile fritters onto salad leaves and garnish with shredded spring onion and lime twists. Serve immediately, as a starter.

Serves 4-6.

Prawn & Leek Timbales

4 leeks
250 g (8 oz) peeled prawns, thawed if frozen
1 teaspoon chopped dill
pinch of grated nutmeg
2 egg whites
2 tablespoons double (thick) cream
salt and pepper, to taste
125 ml (4 fl oz/½ cup) fish stock and white wine
mixed
1 shallot, finely chopped
125 g (4 oz) unsalted butter, in small pieces
1 teaspoon black peppercorns, lightly crushed
TO GARNISH:
4 whole cooked prawns in shell
4 sprigs of dill

1 Preheat oven to 190C (375F/Gas 5). Cut leeks in half lengthwise. Blanch in boiling salted water for 1-2 minutes until slightly softened, then refresh under running cold water.

Line the base and sides of 4 small buttered moulds or ramekins with the leeks, arranging the pieces like the spokes of a wheel and allowing them to overhang the edge of the dishes.

2 Place prawns, dill, nutmeg, egg whites, cream, salt and pepper in a blender or food processor and process until smooth. Fill prepared moulds with the mixture; fold leek strips over to enclose, trimming if necessary. Place in a baking tin half filled with hot water and bake in the oven for 15-20 minutes, until firm.

3 Place stock mixture and shallot in a small pan, bring to the boil and boil rapidly until reduced to about 2 tablespoons. Reduce heat to very low and whisk in butter piece by piece, until smooth and glossy.

Turn the timbales out onto 4 warmed plates and pour the sauce around them. Sprinkle with crushed peppercorns and garnish with prawns and dill. Serve as a starter.

Serves 4.

Prawn & Watercress Rolls

1 egg yolk
½ teaspoon Dijon mustard
salt and pepper, to taste
155 ml (5 fl oz/⅔ cup) olive oil and sunflower oil
mixed
1 tablespoon lemon juice
30 g (1 oz) watercress, chopped
1 stick celery, finely chopped
250 g (8 oz) peeled prawns, thawed if frozen
12 slices smoked salmon
TO GARNISH:
curly endive
orange slices

1 In a bowl, blend egg yolk, mustard, salt and pepper; add oil drop by drop, beating thoroughly between each addition. As mayonnaise thickens, increase the flow of oil to a slow steady stream, beating constantly. Beat in lemon juice and check seasoning.

2 Stir in watercress, celery and prawns. Lay smoked salmon slices on a work surface. Spoon equal amounts of filling onto each slice.

3 Roll up salmon carefully, enclosing the prawn filling. Arrange 2 salmon rolls on each plate and garnish with curly endive and orange slices. Serve with brown bread and butter, as a starter or light lunch.

Serves 6.

Prawns in Noodle Baskets

90 g (3 oz) bean thread (cellophane) noodles
sunflower oil for frying
2.5 cm (1 in) slice cucumber
60 g (2 oz) unsalted butter
1 clove garlic, crushed
250 g (8 oz) peeled prawns, thawed if frozen
2 tablespoons lemon juice
2 tablespoons snipped chives
salt and pepper, to taste
2 tablespoons brandy

1 Divide noodles into 4 equal heaps using scissors or a sharp knife. In a small saucepan, heat about 2.5 cm (1 in) depth of oil. Carefully add one heap of noodles – it will immediately expand to fit the saucepan. Quickly turn noodles over, cook for a few seconds, then drain well on absorbent kitchen paper. Keep warm while cooking remainder.

2 Cut cucumber into matchstick pieces. In a frying pan, heat butter, add garlic and fry for 1 minute. Add prawns and stir-fry quickly until warmed through. Add cucumber, lemon juice, chives, salt and pepper, and cook for 1 minute.

3 Warm brandy and pour quickly over prawns. Ignite and leave until flames have gone out. Place noodle baskets on 4 individual warmed plates. Spoon prawn mixture into centre and serve immediately, as a starter.

Serves 4.

Buttery Shrimp Boxes

1 large unsliced day-old sandwich loaf
90 g (3 oz) unsalted butter
1 shallot, finely chopped
125 g (4 oz) peeled shrimps
60 g (2 oz) baby button mushrooms
3 tablespoons dry white wine
60 g (2 oz) soft cheese with garlic and herbs
4 tablespoons single (light) cream
salt and pepper, to taste
TO GARNISH:
curly endive
sprigs of dill

1 Preheat oven to 190C (375F/Gas 5). Remove crusts from loaf and cut bread into 4 equal slices. Mark out a square 1 cm (½ in) in from the edges of each slice, then cut down to within 1 cm (½ in) of the base. Pull out the crumbs carefully, making sure the base is kept intact.

2 Melt 60 g (2 oz) butter and brush liberally over the boxes, inside and out. Put on a baking sheet and bake in the oven for 20-25 minutes, until crisp and golden brown.

3 Meanwhile, prepare filling. In a small frying pan, melt remaining butter, add shallot and fry for about 5 minutes, until softened. Add shrimps and mushrooms and fry quickly until heated through and mushrooms are slightly softened. Stir in wine, bring to the boil and cook until reduced by half. Lower heat and stir in cheese until melted. Add cream, salt and pepper and stir well until a thick creamy sauce is formed.

Put the boxes on 4 plates garnished with curly endive. Fill with shrimp mixture and garnish with dill. Serve warm, as a starter.

Serves 4.

Shrimp & Spinach Soufflé

500 g (1 lb) young spinach leaves
grated nutmeg, salt and pepper, to taste
45 g (1½ oz) butter
30 g (1 oz/¼ cup) plain flour
155 ml (5 fl oz/⅔ cup) milk
1 tablespoon lemon juice
60 g (2 oz/½ cup) grated Cheddar cheese
185 g (6 oz) peeled shrimps
3 eggs, separated
4 teaspoons sesame seeds

1 Preheat oven to 190C (375F/Gas 5). Put spinach in a large saucepan with just the water clinging to leaves after washing; season with nutmeg, salt and pepper. Bring to the boil, then cover and cook for 5 minutes, until softened. Drain in a sieve, pressing out as much water as possible. Turn onto a board and chop finely. Drain again, then set aside.

2 In a saucepan, melt butter, add flour and cook for 1 minute. Gradually stir in milk, cooking until thickened and smooth.

Remove from heat and stir in lemon juice, cheese, shrimps, spinach, egg yolks, and salt and pepper; stir well. In a bowl, whisk egg whites until stiff, then fold carefully into mixture.

3 Butter a 1.2 litre (40 fl oz/5 cup) soufflé dish and sprinkle with half the sesame seeds. Spoon mixture into dish and sprinkle with remaining sesame seeds. Put on a baking sheet and bake in the oven for 35 minutes, until well risen and golden brown. Serve immediately, with a salad, as a starter or light lunch.

Serves 4.

Shrimp Fettucine

30 g (1 oz) prosciutto
12 basil leaves
90 g (3 oz) unsalted butter
2 cloves garlic, crushed
125 g (4 oz) peeled shrimps
375 g (12 oz) fresh green fettucine
30 g (1 oz/¼ cup) grated Parmesan cheese
salt and pepper, to taste

1 Cut prosciutto into julienne strips. Tear basil leaves in half. In a large frying pan, melt butter, add garlic and fry gently for 1 minute. Add prosciutto, shrimps and basil and cook for 2 minutes. Keep warm while cooking pasta.
2 Bring a large saucepan of salted water to the boil, add fettucine and cook for 3 minutes, or until *al dente*; drain thoroughly.
3 Add half the Parmesan, and salt and pepper to the sauce; stir well. Add the fettucine and toss thoroughly to coat with the sauce.

Divide between 4 individual serving plates and sprinkle with remaining Parmesan. Serve piping hot, with a crisp side salad.

Serves 4.

Note: For dried fettucine, use 250 g (8 oz) and cook for 10-12 minutes.

Shrimp Risotto

500 g (1 lb) cooked shrimps in shell
1 bay leaf
few celery leaves
6 peppercorns
salt, to taste
few saffron threads
90 g (3 oz) butter
1 onion, chopped
1 clove garlic, crushed
375 g (12 oz/2 cups) Italian risotto rice
315 ml (10 fl oz/1¼ cups) dry white wine
2 courgettes (zucchini), cut into sticks
185 g (6 oz) oyster mushrooms, cut into pieces
2 tablespoons chopped parsley
4 tablespoons grated Parmesan cheese

1 Peel shrimps: gently pull off the tail shell and twist off the head; set aside. Wash shells, then put in a saucepan with bay leaf, celery leaves, peppercorns, salt, saffron and 940 ml (30 fl oz/3¾ cups) water. Bring to the boil, then simmer for 20 minutes. Strain and reserve stock.

2 In a heavy-based saucepan, melt half the butter, add onion and garlic and fry gently for about 5 minutes, until softened but not coloured. Add rice and stir to coat all the grains with butter. Add one third of the reserved stock and bring to the boil, then simmer, uncovered, until stock is absorbed. Gradually add more stock and wine until it has all been absorbed and the rice is cooked; this will take about 20 minutes.

3 In a separate pan, melt remaining butter, add shrimps, courgettes (zucchini) and mushrooms and cook for 2-3 minutes. Fold into rice, with parsley and half the Parmesan; check seasoning.

Serve piping hot, sprinkled with remaining Parmesan.

Serves 4.

Dublin Bay Prawns & Wild Rice

16-24 cooked small Dublin Bay prawns
185 g (6 oz/1¼ cups) long-grain rice
60 g (2 oz/¼ cup) wild rice
60 g (2 oz) butter
2 teaspoons chopped tarragon
2 teaspoons snipped chives
1 clove garlic, crushed
2 tablespoons sunflower oil
1 courgette (zucchini), cut into thin sticks
1 carrot, cut into thin sticks
½ teaspoon cumin seeds
125 g (4 oz) oyster mushrooms, cut into pieces
125 ml (4 fl oz/½ cup) fish stock
salt and pepper, to taste

1 Rinse Dublin Bay prawns, then remove shells: twist off the head, then gently pull off the tail shell and remove the body shell. Cut down the back and remove dark vein. Dry well with absorbent kitchen paper; set aside.

2 Cook both rices in boiling salted water for 10-12 minutes, until just tender; drain.

In a small bowl, blend butter, tarragon, chives and garlic together; set aside.

3 In a frying pan, heat half the oil, add Dublin Bay prawns and stir-fry quickly, until they have turned pink. Remove from pan and keep warm. Heat remaining oil in pan, add courgette (zucchini) and carrot sticks and stir-fry for 1-2 minutes. Add cumin seeds and mushrooms and stir well.

Add rice, prawns, stock, and salt and pepper, bring to the boil, cover and cook gently for 2-3 minutes, until prawns are firm.

Just before serving, stir in the herb butter; alternatively, serve prawn mixture on individual plates, topped with a knob of herb butter.

Serves 4.

Note: Dublin Bay prawns are also called langoustines in France, and scampi in Italy.

Seafood Skewers & Mango Sauce

750 g (1½ lb) cooked small langoustines
1 tablespoon olive oil
1 tablespoon lemon juice
1 tablespoon chopped fennel
1 tablespoon chopped parsley
salt and pepper, to taste
1 ripe mango
8 rashers streaky bacon, rinds removed
8 spring onions
1 tablespoon clear honey
1 teaspoon sweet chilli sauce
1 clove garlic, crushed
4 tablespoons freshly squeezed orange juice
1 teaspoon soy sauce

1 Peel langoustines, leaving tail section intact: twist off the head and carefully remove the body shell. Cut down the centre back and remove dark vein.

In a bowl, mix together oil, lemon juice, fennel, parsley, salt and pepper. Add langoustines and stir well. Chill while preparing remaining ingredients.

2 Peel mango and cut in half, along one side of stone; remove stone. Cut one half into 16 cubes. Cut each bacon slice in half and wrap round a mango cube. Halve spring onions.

3 Thread marinated langoustines, bacon-wrapped mango and spring onions onto 8 small skewers.

Roughly chop remaining mango and put in a blender or food processor with honey, chilli sauce, garlic, orange juice and soy sauce. Blend until smooth; transfer to a saucepan and heat through gently.

Put the seafood skewers under a preheated moderate grill and cook for 6-8 minutes, turning occasionally, until langoustines are cooked and bacon is crisp. Serve hot with mango sauce.

Serves 4.

Note: Langoustines are the same species as Dublin Bay prawns and scampi.

Langoustine & Pear Salad

24-32 live langoustines
1 beefsteak tomato, skinned and seeded
1 teaspoon chopped basil
3 tablespoons Greek set yogurt
salt and pepper, to taste
2 small ripe pears
2 teaspoons lemon juice
corn salad
radicchio
curly endive
lettuce heart
TO GARNISH:
sprigs of chervil

1 Bring a large pan of well salted water to the boil, add langoustines, cover and cook for 10-12 minutes, depending on size. Drain, cool, then remove shells: twist off the head, gently pull off the tail shell and remove body shell. Cut down the back and remove dark vein.

2 Finely chop tomato; set half aside for garnish. Put the other half in a blender or food processor with the basil, yogurt, salt and pepper; blend until smooth.

Peel, core and thinly slice pears. Place half a sliced pear on each serving plate and brush with lemon juice. Arrange the langoustines alongside. Place a few salad leaves on each plate.

3 Pour a little tomato cream over the shellfish and top with a little chopped tomato. Garnish with chervil and serve as a starter or light lunch.

Serves 4.

Grilled Lobster

2 x 750 g (1½ lb) live lobsters
2 teaspoons green peppercorns
125 g (4 oz) unsalted butter
2 tablespoons finely chopped parsley
1 tablespoon chopped mixed herbs (basil, tarragon, dill, mint)
2 teaspoons lemon juice
salt and pepper, to taste
TO GARNISH:
salad leaves

1 Secure lobster claws with rubber bands. To prepare each lobster, hold underside down on a board. Place the point of a strong knife on the shell in the centre of the cross-shaped mark between the eyes, and plunge it quickly down through the body. The lobster will be killed instantly. Cut along the body and tail firmly to split the lobster in half.
2 Remove the gravel sac near the head, and black intestinal thread which runs the length of the body. Take out the grey-green liver, and coral if any; these can be used in sauces. Carefully rinse and dry lobsters.
    Crush peppercorns coarsely and mix with butter, herbs, lemon juice, and salt and pepper. Dot half the butter over lobster flesh. Shape the rest into a roll, wrap in foil and chill.
3 Preheat grill to hot setting. Slit underside of lobsters in several places. Cook lobster halves under grill for 12-15 minutes, until flesh is opaque. Slice butter roll and arrange on lobster flesh. Serve on a bed of salad leaves, as a starter or light lunch.

Serves 4.

Note: This sophisticated dish may alternatively be served as a main course for two.

Lobster Salad & Sesame Dressing

4 x 500 g (1 lb) live lobsters
salt and pepper, to taste
DRESSING:
1 tablespoon sesame oil
2 tablespoons olive oil
½ teaspoon Dijon mustard
2 teaspoons white wine vinegar
salt and pepper, to taste
30 g (1 oz/2 tablespoons) toasted sesame seeds
TO SERVE:
2 carrots
1 small celeriac
snipped chives

1 Secure lobster claws with rubber bands. Put lobsters, head down, in a large pan of fast boiling well-salted water. Cover, bring to the boil and simmer for 12 minutes until shells are bright red. Remove from pan, place on a board and leave until cool enough to handle.

Snap off legs and break each apart at the central joint; remove flesh with a skewer. Snap each claw free near the body, then crack the claw shells with a mallet and remove flesh in one piece if possible.

2 With the lobster on its back, cut down either side of the shell, then pull away the boney covering which protects the underside. Prise the flesh free in one piece, starting at the tail. Discard the gravel sac near the head and the dark intestinal thread which runs the length of the body. Take out the grey-green liver, and coral if any; these can be used in sauces.

3 Rinse and dry lobster shells and place on 4 individual serving plates. Slice tail meat into medallions and arrange in the shells with remaining meat. Mix together dressing ingredients and pour over lobster. Shred carrots and celeriac; place a little on each plate and sprinkle with chives. Serve as a starter or light meal.

Serves 4.

Lobster Filo Parcels

60 g (2 oz) butter
2 tablespoons chopped watercress
salt and pepper, to taste
185 g (6 oz) lobster meat
8 sheets filo pastry
melted butter for brushing
TOMATO SAUCE:
500 g (1 lb) ripe tomatoes
1 teaspoon tomato purée (paste)
pinch of sugar
8-10 basil leaves
TO GARNISH:
snipped chives and lemon twists

1 Preheat oven to 200C (400F/Gas 6). In a bowl, blend together butter, watercress, and salt and pepper. Roughly chop lobster meat. Brush one sheet of filo pastry with melted butter; fold in half and brush again with butter. Put a little lobster meat near one short edge and spread with watercress butter.

2 Roll up pastry to enclose lobster, tucking in the ends to form a parcel. Repeat with remaining filo pastry, lobster and watercress butter. Place the parcels on a greased baking sheet and brush again with melted butter.

Bake in the oven for 15 minutes, until golden brown.

3 To make sauce, skin, seed and chop tomatoes. Put in a saucepan with tomato purée (paste), sugar, and salt and pepper; simmer gently for about 15-20 minutes, until thickened. Tear basil leaves roughly and stir into sauce.

Arrange 2 lobster parcels and a little tomato sauce on each serving plate and sprinkle chives over sauce. Garnish with lemon twists and serve as a light meal.

Serves 4.

Lobster & Spinach Roulade

500 g (1 lb) fresh spinach
pinch of grated nutmeg
30 g (1 oz/¼ cup) grated Parmesan cheese
4 eggs, separated
salt and pepper, to taste
FILLING:
30 g (1 oz) butter
30 g (1 oz/¼ cup) plain flour
250 ml (8 fl oz/1 cup) milk
2 tomatoes, skinned and seeded
185 g (6 oz) cooked lobster meat
2 teaspoons chopped dill
2 tablespoons lime juice

1 Preheat oven to 190C (375F/Gas 5). Grease and line a 28 x 18 cm (11 x 7 in) Swiss roll tin.

Put spinach in a saucepan with just the water clinging to the leaves after washing. Cover and cook for 5 minutes, until softened. Drain well, pressing out as much water as possible. Chop finely, then place in a bowl with nutmeg, Parmesan cheese, egg yolks, and salt and pepper; mix well.

In a bowl, whisk egg whites until stiff, then fold into spinach mixture. Pour into prepared tin; shake to level mixture. Bake in the oven for 15 minutes, until firm.

2 Meanwhile, make filling. In a saucepan, melt butter, add flour and cook for 1 minute. Gradually add milk, stirring until thickened and smooth. Simmer for 2 minutes. Chop tomatoes and lobster; stir into sauce with dill, lime juice, and salt and pepper to taste; heat through.

3 Invert the roulade onto a sheet of greaseproof paper and carefully remove lining paper. Cover with filling and roll up from a short edge, using the greaseproof paper to lift the roulade.

Cut into slices and serve warm, as a light meal or starter.

Serves 4-6.

Lobster with Hollandaise

2 carrots, sliced
2 onions, sliced
bouquet garni
440 ml (14 fl oz/1¾ cups) white wine
few fennel stalks
few black peppercorns
2 x 750 g (1½ lb) live lobsters
HOLLANDAISE SAUCE:
2 eggs
2 tablespoons lemon juice
salt, to taste
2 teaspoons pink peppercorns, crushed
185 g (6 oz) unsalted butter

1 In a large saucepan, put carrots, onions, bouquet garni, wine, fennel, peppercorns and 500 ml (16 fl oz/2 cups) cold water. Bring to the boil, then simmer for 5 minutes. Bring to a fast boil, add lobsters, cover and bring back to the boil. Cook for 18 minutes, or until shells are bright red. Lift onto a board.

2 Meanwhile, make sauce. Put eggs, lemon juice, salt and peppercorns in a blender or food processor and blend for a few seconds. Heat butter until foaming; pour half into blender or food processor and blend for a few seconds. Pour in remaining butter and blend for 5-7 seconds, until thick and creamy. Pour into a heatproof bowl over a saucepan of hot water and leave until thickened, stirring occasionally.

3 To prepare each lobster, lay on its back and, using a strong sharp knife, cut through firmly from head to tail end to split lobster in half; separate lobster halves. Discard the gravel sac near the head and the dark intestinal thread running the length of the body. Take out the liver and any coral.

Arrange the lobster halves on individual serving plates and spoon the sauce over the meat. Serve, as a light meal, with salad.

Serves 4.

Lobster Tails in Sorrel Sauce

8 lobster tails
500 ml (16 fl oz/2 cups) fish stock
125 ml (4 fl oz/½ cup) dry white wine
60 ml (2 fl oz/¼ cup) dry vermouth
250 ml (8 fl oz/1 cup) double (thick) cream
1 tablespoon lemon juice
salt and pepper, to taste
60 g (2 oz) butter, softened
250 g (8 oz) young sorrel leaves, shredded
TO GARNISH:
orange slices

1 Place lobster tails top side down on a board and, using a strong sharp knife, cut through the lobster tails, splitting them in two. Discard the dark intestinal vein and remove the meat from the shells in one piece. Rinse well and dry on absorbent kitchen paper.
2 In a saucepan, boil stock, wine and vermouth until reduced to 250 ml (8 fl oz/1 cup). Add cream and simmer until reduced again to the same amount. Add lobster tails and cook gently for 5 minutes; remove with a slotted spoon and keep warm.
3 Add lemon juice, salt and pepper to the sauce. Beat in butter, a little at a time. Add sorrel and cook until just wilted.
Arrange lobster tails on 4 individual warmed serving dishes and pour over the sauce.
Garnish with orange slices and serve as a light meal.

Serves 4.

Strawberry-dressed Crayfish

250 ml (8 fl oz/1 cup) dry white wine
1 small onion, chopped
1 carrot, chopped
1 leek, chopped
1 stick celery, chopped
bouquet garni
salt and pepper, to taste
1 kg (2 lb) freshwater crayfish
STRAWBERRY DRESSING:
125 g (4 oz) strawberries
2 tablespoons grapeseed oil
3 tablespoons lemon juice
1 teaspoon coarse grain mustard
TO SERVE:
salad leaves (lollo rosso, curly endive, chicory)

1 Put wine, onion, carrot, leek, celery, bouquet garni, salt and pepper, and 500 ml (16 fl oz/2 cups) cold water in a large saucepan, bring to the boil and simmer for 5 minutes. Add crayfish, cover and cook for 5 minutes or until they turn pinky-red all over. Drain and cool.

2 Reserve 4 crayfish in shells for garnish. Peel the rest, by carefully twisting off the heads and peeling away the tail shells.

Arrange salad leaves on 4 individual plates and place crayfish on top. Set the reserved crayfish to one side of the plate.

3 To make dressing, press strawberries through a sieve into a bowl. Add oil, lemon juice, mustard, salt and pepper; mix well. Drizzle over the salad to serve.

Serves 4.

Crayfish Salad

20 live freshwater crayfish or yabbies
1 pink grapefruit
125 g (4 oz) French beans, halved
250 g (8 oz) thin asparagus spears
1 ripe beefsteak tomato
1 ripe avocado
8 oyster mushrooms
4 large lettuce leaves
1 orange
125 g (4 oz) unsalted butter
1 teaspoon Dijon mustard
salt and pepper, to taste

1 Put crayfish or yabbies in a large saucepan, cover with water, bring to the boil, then simmer for about 5 minutes, until they turn pinky-red all over. Drain, then leave to cool. Set aside 4 crayfish for garnish. Shell the rest, twisting off the heads and peeling away the tail shells; set aside.

2 Remove peel and white pith from grapefruit; cut between membrane into segments, over a bowl.

Blanch beans and asparagus in boiling water for 4 minutes, then cool quickly under running cold water. Skin, seed and finely chop tomato. Peel, quarter and thinly slice avocado. Wipe mushrooms.

3 Place lettuce on 4 individual serving plates. Arrange vegetables on plates, alternating colours and placing a few grapefruit segments in centre.

Squeeze the juice from the orange and put in a small saucepan with butter, mustard, salt and pepper. Heat gently until butter has melted, whisking constantly. Add crayfish or yabbies and heat through briefly. Remove crayfish or yabbies with a slotted spoon and arrange on the lettuce. Pour over the sauce, garnish with reserved whole crayfish and serve immediately.

Serves 4.

Crab & Orange Salad

2 x 750 g (1½ lb) crabs, freshly boiled (see page 44)
1 head of chicory
2 oranges
90 g (3 oz) alfalfa sprouts
few leaves curly endive
ORANGE DRESSING:
2 tablespoons freshly squeezed orange juice
2 teaspoons Japanese soy sauce
2 tablespoons sunflower oil
1 tablespoon lemon juice
1 tablespoon walnut oil
salt and pepper, to taste
TO GARNISH:
shredded spring onion tops

1 Place crabs shell down on a work surface. Twist off claws and legs. Crack shell of each claw and extract meat. Break apart the legs and remove meat with a skewer. Twist free the bony tail flap on underside of crab and discard.

2 Insert a strong knife between main shell and underside and prise upwards to detach the underside. Scoop out and reserve meat from main shell, discarding the small greyish-white stomach sac and its appendages, just behind the crab's mouth.

3 Pull away the soft grey feathered gills along the edges of the underside and discard. Using a heavy knife, split the underside down the middle; remove flesh from the crevices using a skewer.

Separate chicory leaves; peel and segment oranges, discarding all white pith. Arrange chicory and orange segments alternately in fan shapes on 4 individual plates. Place the alfalfa and curly endive at the base; pile crab meat on top.

Put dressing ingredients in a screw-top jar, shake well and pour over the salad. Sprinkle crab with shredded spring onion and serve as a starter.

Serves 4.

Potted Crab & Summer Vegetables

1 kg (2 lb) crab, freshly boiled (see page 44)
125 g (4 oz) unsalted butter
¼ teaspoon powdered mace
¼ teaspoon ground allspice
2 pinches cayenne pepper
freshly ground black pepper
50 g (2 oz) clarified butter (see below)
4 sprigs of tarragon
8 heads of baby corn
8 asparagus tips
60 g (2 oz) mange tout (snow peas)
oak leaf lettuce
curly endive
2 tablespoons lemon vinaigrette

1 Remove crab meat from shell (see opposite page). Put white and brown meat in a bowl and fork over to mix. In a saucepan, melt butter, add crab, mace, allspice, cayenne and black pepper; mix well.

2 Divide mixture between 4 ramekin dishes, pressing down lightly. Heat clarified butter and pour gently over the top. Garnish with tarragon. Cool, then chill for about 2 hours, until firm.

3 Blanch corn, asparagus and mange tout (snow peas) in boiling salted water for 1 minute. Cool quickly under running cold water; drain well. Place ramekin dishes on 4 large plates and surround with salad leaves and vegetables. Just before serving, drizzle a little vinaigrette over each salad. Serve with fingers of wholemeal toast as a starter or light lunch.

Serves 4.

Clarified butter: Melt 125 g (4 oz) salted butter in a pan, then heat until foaming stops, without browning. Let stand until deposits have sunk to bottom, leaving clear yellow liquid. Strain liquid carefully through muslin into a bowl.

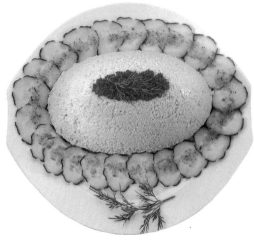

Crab Mousse with Cucumber

250 g (8 oz) crab meat (white and brown)
1 tablespoon lemon juice
¼ teaspoon finely grated lemon rind
4 tablespoons fish stock or water
15 g (½ oz/5 teaspoons) powdered gelatine
375 g (12 oz/1½ cups) curd cheese
1 tablespoon dry sherry
salt and pepper, to taste
2 egg whites
1 cucumber
1 tablespoon chopped dill
1 tablespoon white wine vinegar
1 teaspoon Dijon mustard
2 tablespoons grapeseed oil
TO GARNISH:
sprigs of dill and red lumpfish roe

1 In a bowl, fork together brown and white crab meat, with lemon juice and rind. Put stock or water in a small bowl standing in a pan of very hot water. Sprinkle over gelatine and leave until dissolved.

2 Put crab, dissolved gelatine, curd cheese, sherry and pepper in a blender or food processor and blend until smooth. Taste and add salt if necessary. Turn into a bowl. Whisk egg whites until stiff, then fold into crab mixture.

Turn mixture into a wetted 940 ml (30 fl oz/3¾ cup) mould and smooth the top. Chill the mousse for about 4 hours, until set.

3 Cut grooves along the cucumber skin with a canelle knife, then slice thinly. In a small bowl, whisk dill, vinegar, mustard, oil, salt and pepper together until smooth.

Turn crab mousse out onto a serving plate and arrange overlapping slices of cucumber around the edge. Drizzle the dressing over the cucumber and garnish with dill and lumpfish roe. Serve as a starter or light meal.

Serves 4-6.

Devilled Crab

4 x 500 g (1 lb) crabs, freshly boiled (see page 44)
1 small onion
60 g (2 oz) button mushrooms
1 stick celery
60 g (2 oz) butter
1 teaspoon horseradish sauce
2 teaspoons Dijon mustard
1 tablespoon Worcestershire sauce
15 g (½ oz/6 teaspoons) plain flour
2 tablespoons dry white wine
2 tablespoons double (thick) cream
salt and pepper, to taste
30 g (1 oz/½ cup) breadcrumbs, toasted
1 tablespoon grated Parmesan cheese
TO GARNISH:
snipped chives

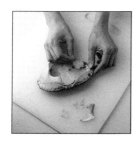

1 Remove crab meat from shells (as described on page 96). When all the meat has been removed, break away the shell edge along the natural dark rim of the shell. Scrub shells thoroughly.

2 Finely chop onion, mushrooms and celery. In a frying pan, melt half the butter, add the vegetables and fry gently for about 5 minutes, until softened. Add horseradish, mustard and Worcestershire sauce and stir well.

Stir in the flour and cook for 1 minute, stirring. Stir in wine and cream and cook, stirring, until thickened and smooth. Remove from heat and fold in crab meat; season with salt and pepper.

3 Preheat grill to medium. Divide mixture between crab shells and sprinkle with breadcrumbs and cheese. Place under preheated grill for 3-4 minutes, until golden brown.

Serve warm, topped with chives and accompanied by a salad.

Serves 4.

Crab Ravioli with Baby Corn

RAVIOLI DOUGH:
250 g (8 oz/2 cups) strong white flour
½ teaspoon salt
2 eggs, beaten
1 tablespoon olive oil
FILLING:
315 g (10 oz) crab meat (white and brown)
30 g (1 oz) butter
few drops of chilli sauce
SAUCE:
90 g (3 oz) butter
185 g (6 oz) baby corn
2 tablespoons lemon juice
12 small basil leaves
TO SERVE:
grated Parmesan cheese

1 To make dough, sift flour and salt onto a work surface; make a well in the centre and add eggs and oil. Gradually mix in flour to form a soft dough; knead for 10 minutes. Wrap in foil and leave for 1 hour.

2 Meanwhile, prepare filling. Flake crab meat into a bowl. Melt butter and add to crab with chilli sauce, and salt and pepper to taste.

On a floured surface, roll out half the dough to a 40 cm (16 in) square. Using a knife, mark the dough into 5 cm (2 in) squares; do not cut right through. Put a little crab mixture in the centre of each square. Brush along the edges of each square with water.

Roll out remaining dough to the same size and place over the filling. Press down between the filling to seal the squares, then cut into pockets. Cook in plenty of boiling salted water for 3-4 minutes; drain and keep warm.

3 To make sauce, in a saucepan, melt butter, add corn and cook, stirring, for 2-3 minutes. Stir in lemon juice, basil, and salt and pepper to taste.

Arrange the ravioli on 4 warmed individual plates and pour the sauce over the top. Sprinkle with Parmesan and serve immediately.

Serves 4.

Crab Burritos

1 tablespoon oil
1 small onion, finely chopped
500 g (1 lb) tomatoes, skinned and chopped
1 tablespoon tomato purée (paste)
¼ teaspoon cayenne pepper
1 teaspoon paprika
2 teaspoons Worcestershire sauce
salt and pepper, to taste
8 pancakes or tortillas, fresh or frozen and thawed
185 g (6 oz) fresh white crab meat
60 g (2 oz) mozzarella cheese, grated
shredded lettuce
1 avocado
1 tablespoon lemon juice
4 tablespoons thick sour cream

1 Preheat oven to 180C (350F/Gas 4). Oil an ovenproof dish.
In a saucepan, heat oil, add onion and fry until softened. Add tomatoes, tomato purée (paste), cayenne, paprika, Worcestershire sauce, salt and pepper. Bring to the boil, then simmer, uncovered, for about 20 minutes, until thick and pulpy.
2 Spread a little sauce over each pancake or tortilla, sprinkle with crab meat and mozzarella, then roll up like a parcel, tucking in the ends. Put in prepared dish, cover and bake in the oven for 20 minutes.
3 Place lettuce on individual serving plates. Peel and slice avocado, brush with lemon juice and arrange on the lettuce. Place 2 burritos on each plate and top with the tomato sauce and a spoonful of thick sour cream. Serve any remaining tomato sauce separately.

Serves 4.

Squid & Red Pepper Salad

750 g (1½ lb) small or medium squid
2 tablespoons olive oil
3 red peppers
6 anchovies, halved
1 tablespoon capers
DRESSING:
2 tablespoons wholegrain mustard
4 tablespoons lemon juice
salt and pepper, to taste
2 cloves garlic, finely chopped
125 ml (4 fl oz/½ cup) olive oil

1 Rinse squid, then holding the head just below the eyes, gently pull away from the body pouch. Discard the soft innards that come away with it; carefully remove the ink sac and discard. Pull out the quill-shaped pen, which is loosely attached to the inside of the pouch, and discard.

2 Cut the head from the tentacles just below the eyes; discard head. Cut out the small round cartilage at base of tentacles. The tentacles will be in one piece. In the centre is a long beak-like mouth; remove by squeezing with the fingers.

3 Skin the body pouch by slipping the fingers under the skin and peeling it off. Remove the edible fins on either side of the pouch. Rinse thoroughly under running cold water; dry well.

Slice the squid. In a saucepan, heat oil, add squid and cook gently for 10-15 minutes; leave to cool. Grill red peppers until the skin is charred; peel off skin. Cut peppers in half, remove stalk and seeds and slice thinly. In a salad bowl, mix together squid, red peppers, anchovies and capers. Whisk dressing ingredients together and stir into salad. Leave to marinate for 1-2 hours before serving.

Serves 6-8.

Squid with Vegetable Bundles

750 g (1½ lb) small or medium squid
salt
BATTER:
185 g (6 oz/1½ cups) self-raising flour
1 tablespoon sesame seeds, toasted
oil for deep-frying
TO SERVE:
2 carrots
125 g (4 oz) mooli
3 courgettes (zucchini)
chives
Japanese soy sauce

1 Clean squid (see opposite page), then slice into thin rings. Wash well, sprinkle with salt and leave to drain in a colander for 15 minutes. Dry well with absorbent kitchen paper.

2 Sift flour and a pinch of salt into a bowl. Stir in sesame seeds, then gradually add 250 ml (8 fl oz/1 cup) cold water, beating constantly to form a smooth batter. Add squid and stir until coated.

3 Cut vegetables into thin match-sticks. Place a few sticks of each vegetable together and tie into bundles with a chive.

Heat oil to 180C (350F). Add squid in batches and deep-fry for 1-2 minutes, until golden brown and crisp; drain on absorbent kitchen paper. Serve immediately, with the vegetable bundles and tiny dishes of soy sauce for dipping. Serve as a starter or light meal.

Serves 4.

Squid & Tomato Casserole

1 kg (2 lb) small or medium squid
3 tablespoons olive oil
2 onions, chopped
4 tablespoons brandy
2 cloves garlic, crushed
500 g (1 lb) ripe tomatoes, chopped
250 ml (8 fl oz/1 cup) red wine
bouquet garni
1 teaspoon paprika
dash of Tabasco
salt and pepper, to taste
pinch of sugar
1-2 tablespoons chopped parsley

1 Clean squid (see page 102), then slice thinly. In a frying pan, heat oil, add squid and fry gently for 10 minutes. Remove with a slotted spoon and set aside.

2 Add onions to the pan and fry for 5 minutes, until softened. Add brandy and boil rapidly to evaporate the alcohol. Add remaining ingredients, bring to the boil, then simmer, uncovered, for 15-20 minutes, stirring occasionally, until thickened. Discard bouquet garni.

3 Press the sauce through a sieve, then return to the pan. Add the squid. Bring to the boil, then cover and simmer gently for 45 minutes, until the squid is tender.

Sprinkle with parsley and serve with saffron rice.

Serves 4.

Note: A 425 g (15 oz) can peeled chopped tomatoes can be used in place of fresh tomatoes.

Braised Squid with Olives

750 g (1½ lb) small or medium squid
3 tablespoons olive oil
1 onion, sliced
2 cloves garlic, chopped
750 g (1½ lb) tomatoes, skinned and chopped
1 bay leaf
2 stalks of fennel
185 ml (6 fl oz/¾ cup) dry white wine
salt and pepper, to taste
90 g (3 oz/⅔ cup) stuffed olives
TO GARNISH:
sprigs of fennel

1 Clean squid (see page 102), then slice into rings. Preheat oven to 160C (325F/Gas 3). In a flameproof casserole, heat oil, add onion and garlic and fry gently for 10 minutes, until lightly coloured. Add squid and fry gently for 5 minutes.

2 Add tomatoes, bay leaf, fennel, wine, salt and pepper. Bring to the boil, then cover and cook in the oven for 1¼ hours, until squid is tender.

3 Remove bay leaf and fennel and stir in olives. Reheat gently; check seasoning. Garnish with fennel and serve with boiled rice.

Serves 4.

Stuffed Squid

2 large squid, cleaned
salt and pepper, to taste
4 tablespoons olive oil
½ Spanish onion, finely chopped
250 g (8 oz) spinach, shredded
1 red pepper, chopped
90 g (3 oz/½ cup) long-grain rice
60 g (2 oz/⅓ cup) pine nuts
3 tablespoons raisins
2 tablespoons chopped parsley
1 kg (2 lb) tomatoes, skinned, seeded and chopped
125 ml (4 fl oz/½ cup) dry white wine
1 teaspoon sugar
TO GARNISH:
lemon twists and parsley sprigs

1 Preheat oven to 180C (350F/Gas 4). Oil a shallow ovenproof dish.

Clean squid (see page 102). Rub squid pouches liberally with salt and rinse well under running cold water. Chop tentacles into small pieces.

2 In a saucepan, heat half the oil, add the onion and fry gently for about 10 minutes, until softened; add tentacles and fry for 5 minutes. Add spinach, cover and cook gently for 3-4 minutes, until wilted.

Stir in red pepper, rice, pine nuts, raisins, parsley, salt and pepper. Stir well, then remove from heat.

3 Two-thirds fill squid pouches with the mixture; sew up the ends. Put in prepared dish.

In a saucepan, put tomatoes, wine, remaining oil, sugar, salt and pepper. Bring to the boil, cover and simmer for 10 minutes. Pour the tomato sauce over the squid, cover dish tightly and cook in the oven for 1 hour, until tender.

Remove thread from squid. Cut each one in half and arrange on warmed individual serving plates. Garnish with lemon twists and parsley to serve.

Serves 4.

Greek Octopus Salad

1 × 750 g (1½ lb) octopus
250 ml (8 fl oz/1 cup) robust red wine
2 tablespoons red wine vinegar
2 teaspoons clear honey
2 sprigs of oregano or 1 teaspoon dried oregano
1 clove garlic, crushed
salt and pepper, to taste
125 g (4 oz/¾ cup) black olives
60 ml (2 fl oz/¼ cup) olive oil
2 tablespoons chopped parsley

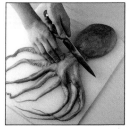

1 Hold octopus firmly by head. Using a sharp knife, cut through flesh below eyes, severing head from tentacles. Turn body pouch inside out and discard innards. Wash well under cold running water. Pick up tentacles; with index finger underneath the centre, push the beak up and cut it away.

2 To tenderize tentacles, beat with a mallet until they feel soft and have lost their springiness. Remove any scales left in the suckers.

Plunge octopus into a pan of boiling salted water for 5 minutes; drain well and leave until cool enough to handle.

Using a sharp knife or scissors, cut octopus into 2.5 cm (1 in) pieces. Put in a saucepan with no extra liquid and heat gently until it produces its own liquid. Increase the heat a little until the liquid has evaporated, then add wine, vinegar, honey, oregano, garlic, salt and pepper. Bring to the boil, cover and simmer for 1 hour, or until tender.

3 Leave octopus in pan until cold, then with a slotted spoon, transfer to a serving dish; add olives. Mix 125 ml (4 fl oz/½ cup) cooking liquid with olive oil and seasoning. Pour over octopus and sprinkle with parsley. Serve with salad leaves.

Serves 4-6.

Peppered Octopus

1 × 500 g (1 lb) octopus, cleaned and boiled (see
page 107)
6 tablespoons olive oil
1 bay leaf
1 small onion, quartered
1 teaspoon black peppercorns
few parsley stalks
2 cloves garlic, finely chopped
2 teaspoons paprika
¼ teaspoon ground chilli
½ red pepper, finely chopped
salt, to taste
TO SERVE:
wedges of lime

1 Using a sharp knife or scissors, cut octopus into 2.5 cm (1 in) pieces. In a large pan, put 1 litre (32 fl oz/4 cups) cold water, 2 tablespoons oil, bay leaf, onion, peppercorns and parsley stalks. Bring to the boil, add octopus, cover and simmer for 1-1¼ hours, until tender. Drain, reserving 125. ml (4 fl oz/½ cup) cooking liquid.

2 In a frying pan, heat remaining oil, add garlic and fry gently for 2 minutes. Add octopus, paprika, chilli, red pepper and salt. Stir well, cover and cook for 2 minutes.

3 Add reserved liquid and cook, uncovered, until slightly reduced. Serve warm with toasted French bread or cold as a salad on a bed of shredded lettuce, accompanied by wedges of lime.

Serves 4.

Octopus in Wine

1 × 1 kg (2 lb) octopus, cleaned and boiled
(see page 107)
2 tablespoons lemon juice
3 tablespoons olive oil
2 teaspoons coriander seeds, crushed
1 onion, thinly sliced
1 leek, thinly sliced
2 cloves garlic, crushed
2 tomatoes, skinned and chopped
1 sprig each of thyme and marjoram
500 ml (16 fl oz/2 cups) dry red wine
2 tablespoons tomato purée (paste)
salt and pepper, to taste

1 Preheat oven to 160C (325F/ Gas 3). Using a sharp knife or scissors, cut octopus into 2.5 cm (1 in) pieces. Put in a bowl with lemon juice and leave for 1 hour.
2 In a flameproof casserole, heat oil, add coriander seeds, onion, leek and garlic and fry gently for 10 minutes.
3 Add octopus and fry, stirring, for 2 minutes. Add tomatoes, herbs, wine, tomato purée (paste), salt and pepper and bring to the boil. Cover the casserole tightly and cook in the oven for 1-1¼ hours, until the octopus is tender. Remove herb sprigs. Serve with rice or steamed potatoes and a crisp green salad.

Serves 4-6.

Octopus in Spiced Coconut Cream

1 × 750 g (1½ lb) octopus, cleaned and boiled
(see page 107)
1 coconut
2 tablespoons sunflower oil
3 tablespoons lemon juice
1 stalk lemon grass
2 slices fresh root (green) ginger
salt and pepper, to taste
2 teaspoons ground cumin
2 teaspoons ground paprika
2 spring onions, shredded

1 Using a sharp knife or scissors, cut octopus into 2.5 (1 in) pieces; set aside.

Pierce the two 'eyes' in the coconut with a sharp skewer and drain off the milk; set aside.

2 Crack open the coconut and remove flesh. Peel off the brown skin. Chop flesh and place in a blender or food processor with reserved coconut milk and 250 ml (8 fl oz/1 cup) cold water. Process until fairly smooth, then strain through a sieve.

3 In a saucepan, heat oil, add octopus and fry quickly until it starts to turn pink. Add lemon juice, cover and cook gently for 10 minutes, then add coconut cream, lemon grass, ginger, salt, pepper and spices. Bring to the boil, then cover and simmer gently for 45 minutes, until octopus is tender; remove ginger and lemon grass.

Transfer to a warmed serving dish and sprinkle with spring onion. Serve with boiled rice.

Serves 4.

Cuttlefish Sofrito

1 kg (2 lb) cuttlefish
2 tablespoons olive oil
1 onion, finely chopped
2 tablespoons chopped parsley
2 tablespoons chopped celery leaves
1 clove garlic, crushed
375 g (12 oz) spinach, shredded
500 g (1 lb) tomatoes, skinned, seeded and chopped
salt and pepper, to taste

1 Wash cuttlefish thoroughly, then place bone side down on a board. Slit the mantle with a sharp knife, open carefully and discard the gut and cuttle bone. Remove the ink sac.
2 Remove the skin from the flaps, then cut the mantle and flaps into 5 cm (2 in) squares; score in a diagonal criss-cross.
3 Cut off tentacles from below the eyes and remove beak. The edible parts of the cuttlefish are the two flaps, mantle and the tentacles.

Chop the tentacles if using.

In a large pan, heat oil, add onion and fry for 5 minutes, until softened. Add parsley, celery leaves, garlic and spinach. Cover and cook for 2-3 minutes, until the spinach has wilted.

Add cuttlefish, tomatoes, and salt and pepper and bring to the boil. Cover and cook gently for 20-30 minutes, until cuttlefish is tender. Serve with boiled rice.

Serves 4.

Fisherman's Soup

1 kg (2 lb) mussels, cleaned (see page 12)
500 ml (16 fl oz/2 cups) dry white wine
30 g (1 oz) butter
1 leek, white part only, chopped
500 g (1 lb) tomatoes, skinned, seeded and chopped
strip of lemon rind
500 g (1 lb) queen scallops, cleaned (see page 16)
salt and pepper, to taste
125 g (4 oz) peeled prawns, thawed if frozen
60 ml (2 fl oz/¼ cup) double (thick) cream
2 tablespoons chopped mixed herbs
(eg, fennel, chives, tarragon, dill)

1 Put mussels in a large saucepan with wine and 250 ml (8 fl oz/1 cup) water. Cover and cook over high heat, shaking pan, for 3-4 minutes, until shells have opened; drain, reserving cooking liquid. Discard any that have not opened. Remove mussels from shells and set aside.
2 In a large saucepan, melt butter, add leek and cook gently for about 5 minutes, until softened. Add tomatoes, lemon rind, half the scallops and 125 ml (4 fl oz/½ cup) reserved cooking liquid. Bring to the boil, then simmer gently for 10 minutes; remove lemon rind. Transfer mixture to a blender or food processor and purée until smooth.
3 Return purée to a clean pan and add remaining cooking liquid. Bring to the boil and season with salt and pepper. Detach corals from remaining scallops and cut the white part of each scallop into 4 pieces. Add scallops, corals, prawns, and mussels to the pan and simmer for 5 minutes. Just before serving, stir in cream and herbs and warm through.

Serves 4.

Variation: Replace mussels with clams.

Seafood Treasure Chest

185 g (6 oz) puff pastry
beaten egg, to glaze
125 ml (4 fl oz/½ cup) dry vermouth
3 egg yolks
185 g (6 oz) butter, melted and cooled
1 tablespoon chopped coriander
salt and pepper, to taste
375 g (12 oz) shelled queen scallops
125 g (4 oz) peeled prawns, thawed if frozen
TO GARNISH:
8 cooked prawns in shell

1 Preheat oven to 220C (425F/Gas 7). On a lightly floured surface, roll out pastry and cut into four 13 x 8 cm (5 x 3 in) rectangles. Put on a dampened baking sheet and slash across top diagonally several times; brush with beaten egg. Bake in the oven for 12-15 minutes, until well risen, crisp and golden brown. Keep warm.

2 In a small saucepan, boil vermouth until reduced by half; cool slightly, then put in a heatproof bowl with egg yolks. Set over a pan of simmering water and whisk together for about 10 minutes, until mixture thickens. Slowly whisk in melted butter to form a sauce. Add coriander, salt and pepper and keep warm over the water.

Steam scallops for 3-4 minutes, until just firm. Add prawns and steam for 1 minute to heat through. Add to the sauce.

3 Split the pastry boxes in half horizontally. Put the bases on 4 individual warmed plates, spoon over the sauce and cover with the pastry lids. Garnish with whole prawns and serve immediately, as a starter or light meal.

Serves 4.

Seafood Terrine

125 g (4 oz) young spinach leaves
750 g (1½ lb) lobster, cooked
3 teaspoons gelatine
250 g (8 oz/1 cup) curd cheese
60 ml (2 fl oz/¼ cup) brandy
2 tablespoons lemon juice
500 ml (16 fl oz/2 cups) double (thick) cream
salt and pepper, to taste
250 g (8 oz) crab meat (white and brown)
1 tablespoon chopped dill
YOGURT SAUCE:
125 ml (4 fl oz/½ cup) natural yogurt
2 teaspoons chopped dill
2 teaspoons chopped mint
TO GARNISH:
sprigs of dill and lemon twists

1 Blanch spinach in boiling water for 1 minute; drain thoroughly and pat dry. Use spinach leaves to line a 1 kg (2 lb) loaf tin or mould, overlapping the edges. Remove lobster meat from shell (see page 32).

Break up shell and put in a saucepan with 185 ml (6 fl oz/¾ cup) water. Simmer for 15 minutes; strain. Sprinkle gelatine over strained liquid, stirring until dissolved.

2 Put lobster meat and half the curd cheese, brandy, lemon juice and reserved liquid in a blender or food processor and blend until smooth; turn into a bowl. Whip cream until soft peaks form and fold half into the mixture. Season with salt and pepper. Turn into prepared mould and smooth the top; chill.

Blend crab meat with remaining cheese, brandy, lemon juice and cooking liquid. Turn into a bowl and fold in remaining cream, with dill, salt and pepper.

3 Pour crab mixture carefully over lobster mixture and smooth. Fold spinach leaves over top to enclose and chill for about 3 hours, until set.

To make sauce, mix together yogurt, dill, mint, salt and pepper. Turn out terrine and cut into thick slices. Garnish with dill and lemon. Serve with yogurt sauce.

Serves 6-8.

Marinated Seafood Skewers

12 scallops
12 small raw scampi, peeled (see page 30)
12 raw king prawns, peeled (see page 26)
2 cloves garlic
2 tablespoons chopped parsley
1 tablespoon torn basil leaves
2 tablespoons lime juice
4 tablespoons olive oil
salt and pepper, to taste
60 g (2 oz/1 cup) breadcrumbs, toasted
TO SERVE:
wedges of lime

1 Rinse scallops, removing any dark strands, and pat dry; detach corals. Cut white part of each scallop into 2 circles. Put in a bowl with scampi and prawns.
2 Finely chop garlic and put in a pestle and mortar with herbs. Pound together to form a paste, add lime juice and pound again. Gradually work in oil to form a thick sauce; season with salt and pepper. Pour over seafood and mix well. Chill for at least 1 hour.
3 Thread scallops, scampi and prawns alternately onto 4 large skewers and sprinkle with breadcrumbs. Cook under a preheated moderate grill for 6-8 minutes, until breadcrumbs are golden and fish is firm; turn several times during cooking. Serve hot, accompanied by rice pilaff, and lime wedges.

Serves 4.

Fritto Misto di Mare

8 raw king prawns
16 cooked scampi
250 g (8 oz) small squid, cleaned (see page 50)
seasoned flour for coating
60 g (2 oz/½ cup) each self-raising flour and
cornflour
½ teaspoon baking powder
salt and pepper, to taste
1 egg, beaten
250 ml (8 fl oz/1 cup) iced water
1 head radicchio
1 small fennel bulb
1 tablespoon pine nuts
2 tablespoons French dressing
oil for deep-frying
lime slices to garnish

1 Shell prawns and scampi, leaving tail section intact. Cut down the back to remove dark vein (see pages 26 and 30). Cut squid pouch and tentacles into thin rings and fins into strips. Toss all seafood lightly in seasoned flour; shake off the excess.

Sift flours and baking powder into a bowl; add salt and pepper. Make a well in the centre and add egg and a little iced water. Beat to incorporate dry ingredients; gradually add more water, beating well, until a smooth light batter is formed.

2 Separate radicchio leaves. Shred fennel and radicchio finely. Arrange salad leaves on the side of 4 individual plates. Sprinkle with pine nuts and drizzle over a little French dressing.

3 Heat oil to 180C (350F). Dip seafood into batter and deep-fry in batches for 2-3 minutes, until crisp and golden. Drain well on absorbent kitchen paper and keep hot, while cooking remainder.

Arrange seafood on the serving plates and garnish with lime slices. Serve immediately, as a starter or light meal.

Serves 4.

Seafood Platter

500 g (1 lb) mussels in shell, cleaned (see page 12)
8-12 oysters
1 tablespoon pink peppercorns
8-12 crab claws
1 cooked small lobster, halved (see page 32)
500 g (1 lb) cooked prawns in shell (see page 26)
RED PEPPER SAUCE:
2 red peppers
2 tablespoons olive oil
dash of Tabasco sauce
salt and pepper, to taste
DILL SAUCE:
1 tablespoon chopped dill
2 tablespoons finely chopped cucumber
1 tablespoon white wine vinegar
185 ml (6 fl oz/¾ cup) thick sour cream

1 Put mussels in a large pan with just enough water to cover. Cover pan and cook over high heat for about 3 minutes, until shells have opened, shaking the pan occasionally. Drain and discard any that have not opened. Leave to cool, then remove the empty half shells.

2 Prise open oysters (see page 14) and sprinkle a few pink peppercorns into each shell. Chill all shellfish and have ready plenty of ice.

To make red pepper sauce, grill peppers under a moderate grill until charred all over. Wrap in foil and leave to cool, then remove skin and seeds and roughly chop flesh. Put in a blender or food processor with oil, Tabasco, salt and pepper, and blend until smooth. Turn into a small serving bowl.

3 To make dill sauce, in a small serving bowl, mix together dill, cucumber, vinegar, cream, salt and pepper.

Arrange the seafood on a large platter with plenty of ice. Serve with the dill and red pepper sauces, and lemon and lime wedges. Thinly sliced dark rye bread is an ideal accompaniment.

Serves 4-6.

Spanish Seafood Stew

500 g (1 lb) mussels in shell, cleaned (see page 12)
12 clams in shell, cleaned (see page 10)
125 ml (4 fl oz/½ cup) dry white wine
salt and pepper, to taste
500 g (1 lb) small squid, cleaned (see page 50)
4 cooked Dublin Bay prawns
3 tablespoons olive oil
1 onion, chopped
2 cloves garlic, crushed
1 tablespoon lemon juice
250 g (8 oz) ripe tomatoes, skinned and quartered
4 tablespoons sherry
250 g (8 oz) peeled prawns, thawed if frozen
1 tablespoon chopped parsley

1 Put mussels, clams, wine, salt and pepper in a large pan. Cover and cook over high heat for about 4 minutes, until shells have opened; discard any that do not open. Strain, then return liquid to pan and boil until reduced by half. Remove the mussels and clams from their shells.

2 Slice squid into rings. Remove shells and dark vein from Dublin Bay prawns (see page 30).

In a saucepan, heat oil, add onion and garlic and fry gently until softened. Add squid and fry gently for 10 minutes. Add lemon juice, tomatoes, reduced cooking liquid, sherry, salt and pepper and bring to the boil. Cover and simmer for 10 minutes.

3 Add Dublin Bay prawns, mussels, clams and peeled prawns; stir and cook for 5 minutes. Sprinkle with parsley to serve.

Serves 4.

Seafood in Cider Sauce

500 ml (16 fl oz/2 cups) dry cider
1 onion, chopped
1 carrot, chopped
bouquet garni
salt and pepper, to taste
1.5 kg (3 lb) mussels in shell, cleaned (see page 12)
750 g (1½ lb) raw king prawns
12 live freshwater crayfish
2 egg yolks
125 ml (4 fl oz/½ cup) double (thick) cream
90 g (3 oz) butter, in pieces
185 g (6 oz) button mushrooms
2 tablespoons lemon juice
TO GARNISH:
sprigs of chervil and croûtons

1 Put cider, onion, carrot, bouquet garni, salt, pepper, and 250 ml (8 fl oz/1 cup) water in a large saucepan. Bring to the boil, then cover and simmer for 10 minutes. Add mussels, cover and cook over high heat for 4-5 minutes, until shells have opened. Remove with a slotted spoon and discard any unopened ones. Remove mussels from shells.

Add prawns and crayfish to the pan and cook for about 5 minutes, until shells are pink. Remove with a slotted spoon and leave until cool enough to handle. Shell crayfish and prawns, leaving on tail shells. Devein prawns. Keep seafood warm.

2 Strain cooking juices into a pan and boil until reduced by three quarters. Blend egg yolks and cream with a little of the cooking juices. Stir into pan and cook gently for 5 minutes, or until thickened; stir constantly and do not allow to boil. Remove from heat and whisk in butter a little at a time, until glossy.

3 Put mushrooms, lemon juice and 2 tablespoons water in a small saucepan and cook gently for about 5 minutes, until softened.

Arrange seafood and mushrooms on a warmed serving plate and pour over the sauce. Garnish with chervil and croûtons to serve.

Serves 4-6.